Youth Retreats

for Any Schedule

Youth Retreats
for Any Schedule

Maryann Hakowski

Saint Mary's Press®

The "Water Relay Race" in the "It's a Miracle" retreat was inspired by John Brazier.

"Where Are Your Clothes Made?" "Finding Nemo," and "Weaving Justice" were designed by Abby Causey, Peace and Justice Minister at Holy Spirit Catholic Church in Virginia Beach, Virginia.

 Genuine recycled paper with 10% post-consumer waste. 5116500

The publishing team included Laurie Delgatto, development editor; Lorraine Kilmartin, reviewer; Mary Koehler, permissions editor; Photodisc/Brushworks, cover image; prepress and manufacturing coordinated by the prepublication and production services departments of Saint Mary's Press.

Interior images by Paul Casper, page 49; and USCC Diocese of Charlotte page, 115

Printed in the United States of America

ISBN 978-0-88489-934-1

Library of Congress Cataloging-in-Publication Data

Hakowski, Maryann.

Youth retreats for any schedule / Maryann Hakowski.

p. cm.

Includes index.

ISBN 978-0-88489-934-1 (pbk.)

1. Spiritual retreats for youth. 2. Church work with teenagers. I. Title.

BV4447.H29355 2007

226'.63—dc22

2006023728

Dedication

In loving memory of Walter Hakowski

May the angels bear you up; give you to drink the holy cup.
May the saints come welcome you; here is a life forever new.
(From Gary Hardin and James Hansen's "Farewell Blessing")

Author Acknowledgments

I wish to thank the following people for their support and assistance in preparing the programs in this book:

- My husband, Mike Hakowski, and my children, Maria, Kyrie, and David, for their patience and time while I was writing this book.
- The teen and adult members of the Youth Advisory Team of Holy Spirit Catholic Church in Virginia Beach, Virginia, who tested many of the ideas and retreats in this book.
- Christina Theisen, Abby Causey, and Kathy Early—champions of peace and justice—who were my inspiration for, and my constant support in, the creation of the "Micah 6:8" retreat.
- Michael Horace and the youth retreat team at the Shrine of Our Lady of the Snows in Belleville, Illinois.

Contents

Introduction

Why Offer a Retreat?

Retreats are a special way to reach out to young people. They are a proven way to be effective in evangelizing and building community. They can be powerful, life-changing events for young people. They are times to get away from daily routines; they include many components of a well-rounded youth ministry program; and they allow time for tackling issues in depth.

A retreat provides an environment for grappling with faith issues and learning new ways to pray. It is an opportunity for young people to celebrate their faith in new and different ways.

Young people and adults have a chance to share their faith stories and build relationships of trust. Young people need and want these relationships with significant adults. Adults want to be approachable to young people and to transmit values and faith. A retreat is a place for sharing the Gospel message. Often, we adults learn as much as young people do.

A retreat is a chance for everyone to have a lot of fun and to play and pray together as one community and one Church.

An Overview of This Book

This book includes five retreats, each designed for a group of twenty-five to forty senior high young people. They are adaptable for smaller or larger groups. One-day, half-day, overnight, and weekend programs are offered. The retreats have a wide variety of topics that speak to the needs and daily experiences of young people.

One of the strengths of these retreats is that they have been tested and improved based on feedback from teens in parish youth groups and Catholic high school classes in Pennsylvania, Virginia, Illinois, and Missouri. Young people have participated in these retreats and have had the opportunity to comment on ways to improve them. In some cases, they have participated in planning the retreats.

An additional strength of these retreats is their flexibility. They can be used as written or they can be adapted to meet particular needs of your group. Individual talks, icebreakers, and discussion activities can be used in the classroom or in other youth ministry settings as well.

The Philosophy Behind the Retreats

The retreats in this book are based on the philosophy that a healthy retreat experience must give retreatants an opportunity to gain a better sense of self, to build relationships with others, and to grow closer to God.

Developing a Better Sense of Self

Most young people in high school are grappling with their self-identity. They are still testing their values and developing character—that is, deciding who they really are. Retreats offer affirmation and opportunities for building self-esteem and identifying personal gifts that can be shared with others.

Building Relationships with Others

Relationships—with peers and with parents or guardians—are a constant concern for young people. By translating the Gospel of Jesus Christ into action for everyday living, retreats can give young people options for daily decisions about relating to others.

Growing Closer to God

Adolescence is a time when young people question, struggle with, and sometimes doubt their faith. They are searching for God but often do not realize it. They are starting to discover the difference between religion and faith and are not sure where they fit in.

Retreats offer teens a comfortable setting for examining and talking about their relationships with God. Retreats are times to deepen those relationships and learn new ways to communicate with God.

Components of the Retreats

Icebreakers

These activities do much more than break the ice. They help participants learn each others' names, stretch their legs and their minds, and learn new skills as they play games. The activities also introduce new segments of a retreat.

Talks

Talks are prepared by both adult and teenage team members. Teenage team members have the authority of a person who is speaking to peers. Their concerns and fears, triumphs and relationships, speak right to the place where young people are. Young people need and want to hear from caring adults, too. Talks also offer an opportunity for a ministry leader, a parent, or a parish priest to share his or her thoughts, feelings, and personal faith stories.

Because speakers truly need to think about and pray about a topic before they begin writing a talk, each speaker can be given a handout relating to his or her specific talk that has a list of points to consider as the speaker prepares. In addition, appendix A, "Helpful Hints for Giving Talks," can be given to speakers.

Creative Activities

Learning through experience is a key ingredient of all the activities in this book. Variety is important. Retreat activities should challenge the imagination and offer different ways for young people to express themselves. Some creative activities include role-plays, dramas, games that teach, videos, skits, art projects, affirmations, and exercises using modern music.

Discussions

As a general rule, retreatants should be assigned to small discussion groups at the beginning of a retreat. When retreatants are asked to find their own groups, they tend to sit with their friends. If you already know the young people, assign groups before the retreat, with a good mix of quiet and outgoing members and being careful to break up cliques or pairs who are likely to disrupt discussions. If you do not know the retreatants, assign them to groups randomly, perhaps breaking up cliques in that way. Some hints for leading small-group discussions are offered in appendix B, "Guidelines for Retreat Team Leaders."

Quiet Time

A mix of short opportunities for reflection with one longer period of quiet during retreats provides beneficial interludes. After each talk, ask the retreatants to take 5 minutes to think and reflect. On all overnight and weekend retreats, each person receives a journal and is asked to write his or her thoughts, feelings, and reactions during these quiet times. The setting for quiet time is important. Whether inside or outside, retreatants need to have room to spread out and be comfortable.

Liturgies and Prayer Services

A retreat is an ideal opportunity to expose young people to a variety of prayer experiences, to expand their personal repertoire of ways to approach God. Some possibilities for placing prayer within a retreat schedule include a morning and an evening prayer, a reconciliation service, a closing prayer, and a liturgy. Include a variety of prayer forms in your services. Music, Scripture, symbols, storytelling, shared prayer, mime, personal witness, secular stories or poems, traditional prayer, and prayer with motions are a few possibilities.

Prayer Points

A prayer point is a creative introduction to reflection. It is designed to help retreatants think of something in a new way. It is also often an occasion for creative prayer experiences.

Eucharistic Liturgies

Liturgy is often the high point of a retreat. A retreat, by nature, is a celebration of faith, and it is only fitting that we include the Eucharist, the most precious celebration we have as Catholic Christians.

If a priest is not able to join you for the entire retreat, plan to meet with him beforehand and share the theme of the retreat so that he is better able to prepare a homily. Another option is to hold the retreat liturgy at the home parish and invite family and friends to join you.

Preparation

Recruiting and Training a Retreat Team

The team approach to retreat planning allows the retreat coordinator to tap into the varied gifts and talents of several people, benefit from the perspective of both teens and adults, and share the burden of preparation.

Look for a balance of adults and young people. Try to choose adult team members who have experience with retreats. If this is not possible, invite adults who are involved with young people, active in the parish, and comfortable with their faith. Look for teens who are natural leaders in a group, may already be in leadership roles, are comfortable leading activities, and show a willingness to share their faith.

Some tasks for team members include the following:

- meet several times to prepare for the retreat
- lead a discussion group
- give a retreat talk
- serve as leaders of prayer
- participate in all activities
- give directions for activities
- enforce retreat ground rules

Hold three or four team meetings before the retreat. Such meetings are for planning and training, and they foster community, cooperation, and teamwork. Here are possible agendas for a series of four team meetings.

First meeting

- Introduce the team.
- Explain the theme and the goals of the retreat.
- Review the tentative schedule.
- Explain the team responsibilities.
- Review guidelines for working with small groups.

Second meeting

- Explain the purpose and the method of the witness talks.
- Divide responsibility for the talks and the activities.
- Discuss ways to promote the retreat.
- Designate committees for food, liturgy, promotion, and entertainment.

Third meeting

- Practice giving the directions for the retreat activities.
- Allow half the team to practice its talks, while the other half offers evaluations and suggestions.
- Plan the prayer services.

Fourth meeting

- Let the second half of the team practice its talks.
- Finalize the prayer services.
- Review the supply lists.
- Finalize transportation plans.
- Discuss last-minute changes and questions.

Emphasize that team members are also retreatants. All team members, including the adults, are required to participate in all the activities, from icebreakers to liturgy.

Appendix A, "Helpful Hints for Giving Talks," and appendix B, "Guidelines for Retreat Team Leaders," are useful for team members as they prepare for the retreat. Copy and distribute these appendices at a team meeting.

Promoting a Retreat

A great retreat is not going to go anywhere unless you promote it and get the young people in the parish or school excited about it. Here are some possible ways to publicize a retreat:

- **Personal contact:** Teen team members can call, write, or e-mail students or young people or invite them after class, at youth ministry gatherings, and after Mass.
- **Mailings:** Send a letter, a flyer, or a formal invitation to every young person in the parish or school, giving all the reasons for attending a retreat.
- **Presentations:** Give a presentation at a youth ministry gathering or in class. Bring along young people who will share their retreat experiences.
- **Sign-up booth:** Set up a sign-up table each Sunday for several weeks. Team members can take registrations and answer questions after Mass.
- **Recruiting parents:** They are your best allies. Tell them about the retreat. Answer all their questions. Ask them to encourage their teens to attend.

Setting

Getting away from the parish or school setting is important for a retreat experience. This is preferable for daylong retreats, but it is essential for overnight and weekend experiences. Some possible settings include a retreat center, a camp, a cabin in the mountains, a shrine, or an unused convent or school building. Whatever site you consider, look for these necessities:

- adequate bathroom and shower facilities
- comfortable sleeping accommodations with separate facilities for teen males, teen females, adult males, and adult females
- modern kitchen or food service facilities
- spacious meeting rooms
- recreational areas—outdoor sports courts or an open grassy area
- an informal chapel or a small, quiet room with moveable furniture

You may also want to ask about the facility's group rules, the policy on damage, the availability of audiovisual equipment, and other pertinent matters.

Permission Forms and Transportation

Check with the parish and diocesan director of youth ministry on required medical and permission forms for youth trips. All teens must have a permission form and medical form. Each adult at the retreat should also have a medical form.

All adults participating in any way in your retreat program must complete the background checks and safe environment training required by your parish and diocese.

Check also with your parish or diocese on regulations for transporting teens. As a rule, no one under twenty-one years of age is permitted to transport teens. Under no circumstances should teens transport other teens. Make sure all the adult drivers have accurate directions to the retreat location. They should also swap cell phone numbers in case they need to contact one another.

Finances

Calculate what the retreat will cost. When determining a budget, include the cost of food, supplies, renting the facility, and transportation. Then determine the cost per person.

In most cases, retreatants must pay for all or part of the cost. Some of the funds may come from the parish budget or the school budget. To keep costs down, you may want to ask for donations of food from parishioners or do some fund-raising. An added benefit of fund-raising is that it promotes the retreat.

Cost should not prevent anyone from attending a retreat. Start a scholarship fund and make the money available when needed.

Meals

You can have the best program in the world, but if the food is poor, your retreat is going to be in trouble. If you are going to a facility where meals are provided, here are some questions you should ask beforehand:

- At what times are the meals served? Is the staff flexible on this?
- What type of food is served? Ask for a menu for each meal you will be served while you are at the facility.
- How large are the portions? Is it possible to have seconds?
- Are provisions made for people who are on special diets? for vegetarians?
- Are snacks provided? in the evening? during the day?

If you will be doing your own cooking and using the kitchen at the facility, you should ask the following questions:

- How large is the kitchen?
- What appliances are available?
- Do we have to bring our own utensils, pots, and dishes?

- What are the guidelines for using the kitchen?
- What happens if we break something?

Seek volunteers from the parish or school to run the kitchen at the facility and prepare the meals. It is difficult for team members, who are running activities and giving talks, to prepare meals. Plan meals that are filling, well balanced, and easy to prepare. Consider preparing some meals in advance and simply heating them at the retreat.

Supplies

Some general supplies are used on most retreats:

- pencils or pens
- a pencil sharpener
- white paper
- construction paper
- poster board and newsprint
- glue or glue sticks
- masking tape and cellophane tape
- index cards
- scissors
- markers
- crayons
- old magazines
- candles
- copies of *The Catholic Youth Bible®* (Winona, MN: Saint Mary's Press) or another Bible
- songbooks or parish hymnals
- liturgy supplies
- large-screen television
- VCR, DVD, and CD players and batteries
- first-aid kit

Make a detailed list of everything you need for the entire retreat and check off things as you prepare. The activities in this book that require specific supplies are accompanied by a detailed list; this will help you in planning. Always bring extra supplies, just in case.

What the Retreatants Should Bring

Give the retreatants a list of what they should bring to the retreat. For a typical retreat weekend, tell participants to bring the following: comfortable clothing appropriate for the time of year, an extra change of clothing and shoes, personal toiletries, sleeping bag, pillow, flashlight, sports equipment, and a snack to share.

You will also want to include a list of things that participants should not bring to the retreat, such as iPods, CD players, cell phones, pagers, electronic games, and other valuables.

Emergencies

Be prepared for emergencies. Before the retreat, make a list of the phone numbers for the nearest police station, rescue squad, and firefighting unit. Make sure you have the name and number of the facility manager, especially if she or he does not live on the property. Find the fire exits so you can point them out to everyone at the start of the retreat.

Locate the hospital nearest to the facility and make sure every adult team member has the phone number and clear directions on how to get there. Make sure you have medical information for each retreatant. The best treatment is prevention. Make sure the facility you use and the activities you choose are a safe environment for retreatants. At least one adult team member should have basic Red Cross training. Check to see if the facility has a first-aid kit. If not, then be sure to bring one.

Discipline

Set a strict code of conduct and stick to it. Guidelines are necessary on retreats to avoid problems and make the stay enjoyable for all.

If you are on a school retreat, the school code of conduct should remain in force. Also check on the rules of the facility you will be using.

Make sure all retreatants know the rules before the retreat. Review the code of conduct again upon arrival at the retreat site, answer questions, and clarify specific rules. It is always a good idea to have parents and teens sign copies of the ground rules when they register for the retreat.

Here is a partial list of retreat ground rules. You can develop other rules with your team.

1. No smoking is permitted.
2. No alcohol or drugs are permitted. Anyone bringing these substances to the retreat will be asked to leave immediately.
3. Cell phones, pagers, CD players, and electronic games should be left at home.
4. All retreatants must stay in designated retreat areas.
5. Any emergency must be reported immediately to an adult.
6. Respect and take care of the building and grounds. Any damage should be reported immediately.
7. Food is permitted only in the cafeteria or canteen.
8. Everyone is responsible for turning off the lights and turning down the heat when leaving a room.
9. Retreatants must be prompt for all activities.
10. Name tags are to be worn for all retreat activities.
11. No boys are permitted in girls' rooms, and no girls are permitted in boys' rooms.
12. A lights-out time will be in effect each night.
13. All rooms and bathrooms should be in order before you leave them.

Traditions

Traditions are fun and a special part of retreats. They are the extra touches that one remembers or treasures for years. Some possible traditions are as follows:

- Ask a volunteer to say grace and allow the people who sit at that table to eat first. (You should not have any trouble getting volunteers after that meal.)
- Have everyone dress up for a candlelight dinner served by the retreat team.
- Distribute medallions, customized T-shirts, or personalized prayer books.
- Give each retreatant a reflection booklet of poems, prayers, and songs compiled by the team. It is important to note that you must follow copyright regulations when copying any printed material. Permission to reprint any copyrighted material must be obtained from the publisher.
- Before the retreat, ask people at the parish or school to write words of encouragement for the retreatants. Give the notes to individuals or to the group throughout the retreat.
- Pick a theme song for the retreat.
- Before the retreat, divide the retreatants into pairs as prayer partners. Give each partner the other partner's name to pray for during the retreat. However, keep the identity of each prayer partner a secret until the sign of peace is made at the closing liturgy.
- Take lots of photos for a retreat album. Pose for a group photo and make sure everyone gets a copy after the retreat.
- Gather with friends and family back at the parish for a noisy, joyful welcome home.

Flexibility and Prayer

After all the planning and preparation that goes into a retreat, add these two things to the retreat list:

- Be flexible.
- Pray!

Expect the unexpected. Every group, every young person, and every retreat is new and different. For that reason, it is best to mark retreat schedules "tentative." Structure is important, but you have to meet the needs and concerns of each individual or group. Be open to change and adapt your approach when needed. Being flexible can go a long way in easing frustration.

Pray. Do it a lot. Do not let the rush of retreat planning brush this aside. Do it before, during, and after a retreat. Be open to the gifts of the Holy Spirit awakening in yourself, the team members, and the retreatants.

Center the retreat on Christ. Think of it as one long, joyous, vibrant, ever-moving, ever-growing prayer to God. Do not be afraid to let go and let God. God is what we are all about and why we do what we do.

Retreat 1

What Is Your Net Worth?

Introduction

"What Is Your Net Worth?" is a day-long retreat for comparing and contrasting society's definition of self-worth with God's definition of our great worth. The retreat may be held at the start of the Lenten season, in September at the start of the school year, or in January at the start of the new year.

Goals

- To help retreatants to grow in self-worth in light of Gospel values.
- To teach retreatants new ways to study and reflect on the Scriptures.
- To encourage retreatants to examine their conscience in light of the Sunday Gospel readings.
- To help retreatants recognize the importance of having a support system and providing a support system for others.
- To challenge retreatants to "cast their nets with Jesus" and grow as Christians in faith and action.

Schedule

The following sequence for "What Is Your Net Worth?" is just one suggestion for arranging the schedule. Use the column labeled "Actual Plan" to record the activities, sequences, and starting times that will work for you.

Time	*Activity Name*	*Activity Type*	*Actual Plan*
9:00 A.M.	Getting Caught Up in Discussion	Community building	______
9:30 A.M.	Gathering and Welcome	Introduction	______
9:45 A.M.	What Is Your Net Worth?	Discussion	______
10:00 A.M.	Break		______
10:15 A.M.	How Does God Define Our Net Worth?	Scripture activity	______
11:30 A.M.	Lunch		______
12:15 P.M.	What or Who Is Your Safety Net?	Sharing and prayer	______
12:45 P.M.	What Is Tangled in Your Net?	Examination of conscience	______
	What Is Caught in Your Net?	Writing project	______
1:30 P.M.	Break		______
1:45 P.M.	Where Do You Need to Cast Your Net?	Quiet time	______
2:00 P.M.	Cast Your Net with Jesus	Networking	______

General Materials and Preparation

- The suggested space needs for this retreat include a large gathering space, tables for small groups, and a designated prayer space.
- Gather the following items:
  - ❑ name tags, one for each retreatant
- Create a portable supply basket for each small group, containing the following frequently used items:
  - ❑ pens or pencils
  - ❑ markers
  - ❑ scissors
  - ❑ glue sticks
  - ❑ self-stick notes
  - ❑ participant journals or blank sheets of paper
  - ❑ songbooks or hymnals
  - ❑ copies of *The Catholic Youth Bible* or another Bible
- Place a basket at each group table.

Detailed Description of Activities

Getting Caught Up in Discussion (9:00 A.M.)

Preparation

- Gather the following supplies:
  - ❑ heavy fishnet that is large enough to cover a small table
  - ❑ a stapler
  - ❑ a small table
  - ❑ a white cloth that is large enough to cover a small table
- Copy the questions found in resource 1, "Questions for the Net," onto a sheet of blue paper and cut the paper into strips. You will need one question for each participant.
- Staple the strips of questions all over the fishnet.
- Place the white cloth on the table, and place the fishnetting, with questions attached, on top of the cloth.

1. As retreatants arrive, invite them to pull one question each from the netting. Ask each person to find a partner and share the answer to the question. When the partners finish, invite them to swap questions and find another partner.

2. Repeat this process until all retreatants have arrived and you are ready for the introduction and welcome.

Gathering and Welcome (9:30 A.M.)

1. Introduce yourself and welcome everyone to the retreat. Thank the retreatants for sharing the net questions during the first activity. Tell them how glad you are that they got "caught up" in getting to know one another and sharing. Encourage them to be open and to continue to share throughout the retreat day. Continue by making the following points in your own words:

> Retreats offer great opportunities for better understanding ourselves, others, and God. This retreat includes Scripture, sharing, prayer, fellowship, and a meal.
>
> During this retreat, we will look at how society views our "net" worth as compared with the great value God places on each one of us. We will learn about the "safety nets" in our lives and how we can be there for others. We will also explore the obstacles that tangle our nets and make it tough to be a disciple of Jesus. Most of all, we will explore ways that each of us can get caught up in the net of discipleship.

What Is Your Net Worth? (9:45 A.M.)

Preparation

- Gather the following supplies:
  - ❑ newsprint
  - ❑ markers
  - ❑ masking tape
  - ❑ two copies of *The Catholic Youth Bible* or another Bible
- Ask two retreatants to prepare to proclaim the Scripture readings: Mark 1:16–20 and John 1:35–42.

1. Begin a large-group discussion with the following questions:

- How do you think society measures your net worth?
- What tools do you and I use to measure worth?
- What would you consider to be the measurements of success?

Record the group's answers on newsprint.

2. Follow up by asking this question:

- What are the dangers of measuring our net worth in these ways?

Again, write the responses on newsprint.

3. Invite the two young people that you have chosen to proclaim the Scripture passages to come forward. The reading from Mark should be proclaimed first. Invite all the retreatants to listen attentively to the Scriptures. Allow retreatants to have a moment or two of silent reflection after each proclamation.

4. Ask the retreatants:

- How do you think Jesus measures our net worth?

Again, record their answers on the newsprint, contrasting them with the answers recorded earlier in the discussion.

5. Close this discussion with a few of the following thoughts:

> If you are still fishing for the topic of this retreat, think back to these readings and remember that in the eyes of God, your worth is immeasurable, especially by any human standards. Come, discover how much God and Jesus value our net worth.

Break (10:00 A.M.)

How Does God Define Our Net Worth? (10:15 A.M.)

Preparation

- Gather the following supplies:
  - ❑ copies of handout 1, "The Steps for *Lectio Divina*: Spiritual Reading," one for each person

1. Introduce the activity in the following way:

> In the first activity, we cast a net of questions to get to know one another better. Then we compared the way society measures worth with the great worth Jesus grants to each of us. Now we turn to the Scriptures to take a deeper look at what God reveals to us.

Invite retreatants to form groups of six to eight people. Assign one adult leader to each group. Invite each group to be seated at a table. Make sure each group has a basket of supplies.

2. Ask the groups to search the Scriptures for examples of how God defines our net worth or of how God does so through Jesus. They should come up with at least one example for each person in their group and list the examples on a sheet of paper.

3. Ask each group to choose one of the Scripture passages for further discussion. Allow a minute or two for them to decide which passage to use. Provide each retreatant with a copy of handout 1. Offer the following information:

> *Lectio divina* is a Latin term that literally means "divine reading" or "sacred reading."
>
> *Lectio divina* is a way of allowing the Scriptures to become again what God intended them to be—a means of uniting us with him.
>
> *Lectio divina* aims to make us aware of God's presence through a five-step process: *lectio, meditatio, oratio, contemplatio,* and *actio:*
>
> - *Lectio* is receiving the word of God.
> - *Meditatio* is allowing the word to be present in our awareness.
> - *Oratio* is sharing ourselves in prayer.
> - *Contemplatio* is resting in the presence of God.
> - *Actio* is responding to God's message with action.

4. Describe the *lectio divina* process as noted on the handout. Then invite the groups to walk through the process together. You might need to remind them of the steps as they go along. Some basic direction is noted here:

- One person reads the Scripture passage aloud and pauses at the end for one or two minutes of silence. During the silence, group members choose a word or phrase that has drawn their attention.
- Each person is invited to share aloud the word or phrase. No elaboration is necessary.
- A different person reads the same passage a second time and pauses for two or three minutes of silence. During the silence, retreatants reflect on

this question: How does the word or phrase that has touched my heart touch my life today?

- Invite retreatants to share their answers aloud.
- A new person reads the passage a third time and pauses for two or three minutes at the end. During the silence, group members reflect on this question: What is Christ calling me to do or become today or this week?
- Invite everyone to share the results of their reflection.
- After full sharing, everyone prays silently for each person in the group.
- Anyone may pass at any time. If a retreatant prefers to pray silently instead of sharing with the group, he or she can simply state this aloud and conclude the silent prayer with an "Amen."

5. When all the groups have had ample time to work through the process, invite them to return to the large group. Ask for a spokesperson from each small group to read the passage the group discovered and share some of what the group learned in praying the passage.

6. Conclude with a discussion of the following questions:

- How was this process for you? Was it helpful?
- Did your experience or interpretation of the Scripture text change throughout the process? If so, how?
- What would be the value of incorporating *lectio divina* into your regular prayer routine?

Be sure to note that with simple adaptations, an individual can use this method just as easily as a group can.

Lunch (11:30 A.M.)

You do not have to serve fish sandwiches for lunch, but let your kitchen crew and table decorating committee have some fun with the menu and table décor so they connect with your retreat theme.

What or Who Is Your Safety Net? (12:15 P.M.)

Preparation

- Gather the following supplies:
  - ❑ masking tape
  - ❑ a long bamboo pole (an old broom handle would also work well)
  - ❑ netting from the previous activity
  - ❑ blue and white yarn, cut into 6-inch pieces, one piece of each color for each retreatant
  - ❑ scissors
  - ❑ newsprint
  - ❑ markers

- With the masking tape, make a long straight line down the center of the meeting space. Arrange half of the chairs on one side of the line and half on the other side.

1. Ask for a volunteer to help with a special demonstration. Take the person aside, give the bamboo pole to him or her, and ask him or her to walk on the masking tape line, pretending to be a tightrope walker. Tell the volunteer to go ahead and have some fun with the charade.

2. Ask the entire group the following question:

- How is walking a tightrope sometimes similar to our everyday lives?

Invite the retreatants to share their answers aloud and then come forward and write their answers on the masking tape line on the floor.

3. Ask for eight volunteers for another demonstration. Take them aside and tell them they have to create, using only themselves as props, a safety net for a tightrope walker. Tell them to be creative and have some fun. Have them perform their act.

4. Now ask the retreatants the following questions:

- What makes tightrope walking challenging?
- What would a person need if, instead of walking on a line of masking tape on the floor, she or he were suspended way up in the air far above our heads?

Summarize the answers to the questions in the following way:

> Sometimes in our everyday lives we feel as if we are walking a tightrope. We have to balance school and work, relationships with family and friends, and school work with other activities. Sometimes the pressures can seem overwhelming, and we lose our balance. Through the support of family and friends and the love of God, we can bring our lives into balance again. Sometimes we are the ones in need of a safety net formed by this network of God and others. Sometimes we are the safety net for others.

5. Give each person a piece of blue yarn and a piece of white yarn. Gather the retreatants in a group around the fishnet. Invite them to be silent for a moment as you begin a prayer experience.

6. Ask each person to pray for someone in need, someone who needs a safety net right now. Explain that retreatants should not pray for an individual by name; rather, they should pray by describing a situation. For example, "I would like to pray for a friend who is struggling with . . ." or "a family member suffering from . . ." Also, give them the option of praying for someone silently if they wish. After they have offered their prayers, invite them to tie their pieces of white yarn to the fishnet. Allow enough time for everyone wishing to participate to do so.

7. For the second prayer, ask retreatants to pray individually for someone who is there when they are in need, someone who is a safety net for them. Invite the young people to tie their pieces of blue yarn to the fishnet after their prayers have been shared. Once again, allow the option of silent prayer.

8. Close by inviting all to hold these people up in prayer for the remainder of the retreat. Then offer this final prayer:

 Lord, we thank you for being our safety net during the tough times of our lives. Bring us closer to you each day so we may find true balance in our lives. Thank you also for the blessing of friends and family members who hold us up. Give us courage to reach out to those in need through word, action, and prayer. We pray this in your Son's name. Amen.

What Is Tangled in Your Net? What Is Caught in Your Net? (12:45 P.M.)

Preparation

- Gather the following supplies:
  - ❑ index cards, one card for each small group
  - ❑ newsprint
  - ❑ markers
- Copy the citations for the Gospel readings for the next several Sundays onto the index cards. You will need one Gospel passage for each small group.

1. Ask the participants the following question:

- What is an examination of conscience?

 Summarize their answers, and then share this definition:

 Prayerful reflection on and assessment of one's own words, attitudes, and actions in light of the Gospel of Jesus; more specifically, the conscience evaluation of one's life in preparation for reception of the Sacrament of Reconciliation. (*The Catholic Faith Handbook for Youth [CFH]*, p. 409)

Continue your comments in this way:

 Although an examination of conscience is most needed when we prepare for the sacrament of Penance and Reconciliation, we can examine our conscience at any time. A retreat is a great opportunity to look at our relationships with God and others and consider how we need to change. The Gospels are full of challenges for us to grow and change.

2. Invite the retreatants to regather in their small groups. Ask each small group to choose one of the upcoming Gospel passages you have written on the index cards. Ask the group members to read the passage individually first. Then ask them as a small group to talk about the questions or challenges found in the passage.

3. Provide each group with a sheet of newsprint and a marker or two. Ask the group members to write down at least five questions that would challenge others to examine their conscience. Use John 9:1–42, the passage in which Jesus heals the blind man, as an example, and offer the following questions as examples:

- Have I harshly judged the actions of others without knowing their motives or their backgrounds?
- Some people who are blind are still able to see God clearly. Why am I not able to see God all the time?
- When was I blind to someone else's needs, paying attention to only my own needs?

Allow about 20 minutes for the groups to complete this task.

4. If time permits, invite a few groups to share the results of their work. Conclude this activity in the following way:

> In our crazy, busy, noisy lives, it is important to make time to reflect on the Scriptures. Taking time to look at the areas in our lives that need some change is important if we are to really remain open to hearing and living the word of God in our everyday lives.

Encourage the retreatants to make a practice of examining their own conscience. Make them aware of the times that the sacrament of Penance and Reconciliation is available at the parish or school.

Break (1:30 P.M.)

Where Do You Need to Cast Your Net? (1:45 P.M.)

Preparation

- Gather the following supplies:
  - ❏ copies of handout 2, "Questions for Quiet Reflection," one for each retreatant

1. Give each person a copy of handout 2. Ask them to read the Scripture passage (John 21:1–14) noted on the handout and to reflect on what they have learned during the retreat so far by spending some quiet time writing their answers to the reflection questions. Ask them to find a quiet space where they will not be distracted or tempted to start a side conversation.

Cast Your Net with Jesus (2:00 P.M.)

Preparation

- Gather the following supplies:
  - ❏ a large ball of brown yarn
- Invite two older teen team members to each prepare a 5-minute witness talk. To help them prepare, give them both a copy of resource 2, "Suggestions for the Cast Your Net with Jesus Witness Talk," as well as a copy of appendix A, "Helpful Hints for Giving Talks."

1. Introduce each team member before he or she gives his or her talk.

2. When the talks are over, thank the team members for sharing and offer any summary comments you think might be helpful.

3. Invite everyone to sit in a circle on the floor. Ask the retreatants to reflect for a few moments on a way they can "cast their nets with Jesus," a way they can begin to put their faith into action. Begin by sharing some examples, such as joining a Bible study group, volunteering at a soup kitchen once a month, or treating parents with kindness. Then pause for a moment. Holding onto the end of the yarn, unroll it and pass the ball to another person, inviting him or her to share an example. Tell the retreatants to continue passing the yarn ball until all have had a chance to share their examples and find a place in the net.

4. Close the activity, and the retreat, by recapping the events of the retreat and offering some challenges for the future. You may want to use these or similar words:

   We began the day by getting caught up in discussion and learning more about the retreat theme and one another. Then we compared society's measurement of self-worth with the immeasurable love of God. We reflected on the Scriptures through the powerful prayer practice of *lectio divina* and also examined our conscience in light of the Scriptures. We learned the importance of supporting one another in word, action, and prayer—that is, by being safety nets.

   What are some challenges we can consider as we leave this retreat today?

Invite the retreatants to share some thoughts. You may wish to offer your own comments throughout the discussion. Be sure to summarize all the points offered before concluding. Close by thanking everyone for their participation and presence at the retreat.

Alternative Ideas for This Retreat

Here are some activities that can be used for a longer version of this retreat or as alternative activities:

- Work with the parish liturgy team or campus ministry team to create a reconciliation service that can be included after the section on examination of conscience. Invite a priest to give a short overview for retreatants who may not have received the sacrament of Penance and Reconciliation for some time.
- Invite a counselor from the local Catholic high school or Catholic Social Services to talk about the importance of getting help for peers who are in trouble. Teens need to know that they should not try to handle serious problems on their own. They need to receive affirmation that they are not betraying a trust if they get help for someone, and they should be told how and where they can go to get help for themselves and others.

Follow-Up Ideas for This Retreat

Here are some ideas for follow-up activities for this retreat:

- Continue networking about Jesus by creating a blog page on the youth ministry Web site, where teens can have a place to share their faith.
- Collect the examinations of conscience created by each group. After some judicious editing, make copies of all the sets and give a copy to each retreatant to use over the next several weeks to help in reflecting on the Gospels proclaimed when a retreatant attends weekend liturgies.

Resource 1

Questions for the Net

Name three different kinds of netting or nets.

Give an example of where nets appear in the Bible.

Have you ever been fishing? Can you share a fish story?

Do you like to go fishing? Why or why not?

Are you better at using a fishing net or the Internet?

What is one measurement of net worth?

How do some people use their appearance to define their worth?

When Jesus looks at you, what do you think he sees?

What is a safety net?

How are you a safety net for others?

What are some things that can get caught in a net?

What can cause a net to get tangled?

What is an examination of conscience?

Where do you need to cast your net?

How do you make quiet time for yourself?

If you could hang a hammock anywhere in the world, where would you hang it?

What is one thing you hope to get out of this retreat?

What do you hope to put into this retreat?

What is your prayer intention for this retreat?

What is your favorite way to pray?

What is your favorite Scripture story? Why?

What is your favorite Scripture verse? Why?

Handout 1

The Steps for *Lectio Divina*: Spiritual Reading

Step 1. *Lectio* (lex-ee-oh), "Reading"

Read the Scripture passage. Try reading it out loud. Try reading it several times. Let the words sink in deeply. Open your mind and heart to the meaning of the words.

Step 2. *Meditatio* (med-it-tots-ee-oh), "Meditation"

Reflect on the Scripture passage. Think deep thoughts. Ask yourself questions such as the following:

- What does this passage say to me?
- Who am I in this passage?
- What do I see? What do I hear?
- What do I think?
- To which character do I most relate?
- What do I most need to learn from this?

Try taking notes on your answers to the questions. Try journaling about the insights you gained from reflecting.

Step 3. *Oratio* (or-ot-see-oh), "Prayer"

Move into the heart of the matter. Feel deep feelings. Consider the following questions as you respond to God:

- What do I want to communicate to God?
- What am I longing for in my relationship with God?
- What do I desire in my prayer life?
- What secrets of the heart are ready to be expressed? Is there joy? Grief? Fear? Gratitude?

Express your intimate self to God in your own personal way.

Step 4. *Contemplatio* (con-tem-plot-see-oh), "Contemplation"

Simply rest in the presence of God. Be passive and just enjoy God. Settle into the tenderness of God's love.

Step 5. *Actio* (ax-see-oh), "Action"

Ask yourself the following questions and answer them with utter honesty:

- How is God challenging me?
- Is there a good thing God is calling me to do?

- Is there a harmful thing God wants me to stop doing?
- What is the next step I need to take?

Decide on a course of action (large or small). Make the commitment and follow through with your plan.

Handout 2

Questions for Quiet Reflection

Read the Scripture passage John 21:1–14, and then reflect on the following questions:

Where do you need to cast your net?

Why are you afraid to cast your net?

What is your net worth as a follower of Jesus?

Resource 2

Suggestions for the Cast Your Net with Jesus Witness Talk

A witness talk is meant to encourage retreatants to get or stay involved with the youth community, take on a greater role in the parish community, and start putting their faith into action. When preparing this 5-minute witness talk, consider the following questions:

- Why is networking important?
- Why do we need to support one another as a youth community?
- What are some ways the retreatants are involved in their parish and youth community?
- Why is it important to put faith into action?

Consider reflecting on the following Scripture passages:

- John 15:1–17
- Matthew 10:1–14
- Luke 14:25–33
- Mark 1:16–20
- Luke 9:1–6

Retreat 2

Many Colors, One God

Introduction

"Many Colors, One God" is a great way to build bridges between retreatants in different parishes or schools, especially if they have different ethnic or socioeconomic backgrounds. It would serve as a good ninth-grade school retreat for all new students. It would also be a great retreat for the start of a new year, when there are many new young people getting involved.

Goals

- To help retreatants understand the value of diversity and how to celebrate it.
- To assist retreatants in identifying diversity issues found in the movies and relating these issues to real-life situations.
- To encourage retreatants to reflect on how Jesus would handle the diversity dilemmas we encounter in everyday life.
- To provide retreatants with opportunities to explore different types of diversity and to reflect on what the world would be like without diversity.
- To help retreatants affirm the knowledge that we are all created in the image and likeness of God.
- To encourage retreatants to work together as a team to build community.

Schedule

The following sequence for "Many Colors, One God" is just one suggestion on how to arrange a schedule. Use the column labeled "Actual Plan" to record the activities, sequences, and starting times that will work for you.

Time	*Activity Name*	*Activity Type*	*Actual Plan*
8:30 A.M.	Gathering Activity	Icebreaker	______________
9:00 A.M.	Welcome and Opening Prayer	Prayer	______________
9:10 A.M.	Sticking Together	Group forming	______________
9:15 A.M.	Hot Potato	Community building	______________
9:45 A.M.	The Color of Diversity	Art project	______________
10:10 A.M.	If We Could All Be the Same	Discussion	______________
10:35 A.M.	What Color Is God?	Discussion	______________
11:00 A.M.	Break		______________
11:20 A.M.	Video Challenges	Video discussion	______________
12:00 P.M.	Lunch		______________
12:30 P.M.	Clue Hunt	Outdoor activity	______________
1:15 P.M.	Break		______________
1:30 P.M.	What Would Jesus Do?	Role-plays	______________
2:00 P.M.	Prayer Patch Tapestry	Craft prayer	______________
2:30 P.M.	Come, All You People	Closing prayer	______________

General Materials and Preparation

- The suggested space needs for this retreat include a large gathering space, tables for small groups, and a designated prayer space.
- Gather the following items:
  - ❑ name tags, one for each retreatant
  - ❑ small round stickers in several colors, enough for each small group of six to eight people
- Divide the larger group into small groups of six to eight and assign a color to each group.
- Before the retreat, create a name tag for each person. Place a small round sticker of one color in the corner of the name tags for each group. When retreatants arrive, give them their name tags.
- Create a portable supply basket for each small group, containing the following frequently used items:

  - ❑ pens or pencils
  - ❑ markers

- ❏ scissors
- ❏ glue sticks
- ❏ self-stick notes
- ❏ participant journals or blank sheets of paper
- ❏ songbooks or hymnals
- ❏ copies of *The Catholic Youth Bible* or another Bible

- Place a basket at each group table.

Detailed Description of Activities

Gathering Activity (8:30 A.M.)

Preparation

- Gather the following supplies:
  - ❏ copies of handout 3, "Me Too," one for each retreatant

1. As the retreatants start to gather, give each a copy of handout 3. Ask them to fill out the right side of the handout by themselves. After more retreatants arrive, encourage them to find someone who has an answer similar to one of theirs. When two people find a match, they should sign the line to the left of the item on each other's sheets. No one should sign a sheet twice.

(This activity is taken from Marilyn Kielbasa, *Community Building Ideas for Ministry with Young Teens,* pp. 53–54.)

2. When you are ready to formally start the retreat day, comment on this activity, explaining that it helped retreatants learn more about one another and about what they have in common with others. They may also have discovered some things that make the group unique. Invite them to continue this discovery throughout the retreat day.

Welcome and Opening Prayer (9:00 A.M.)

Preparation

- Create a prayer table by placing a Bible and a candle on a small table.

1. Introduce the retreat with these or similar words:

> Today is an opportunity to get to know some folks better, a day to discover the many things we have in common. It is also a chance to recognize and celebrate our differences.
>
> Today, together, we will discover that God loves wonderful variety. We will take a peek at a world where everyone is the same and learn a few lessons from M&M's. We will watch a few movie clips and have a chance to reflect on what Jesus would do in situations that we encounter in our own lives.
>
> Today is a chance to work together.
> Today is a chance to build some bridges.
> Today is a chance to learn from our mentor, Jesus.
> Today is a chance to pray for a better world.
> Today is a chance to continue building the Reign of God.

So fasten your seat belts. Be ready for anything. Take an active part in everything we do—and I assure you that you will be surprised at what you discover.

2. Create an atmosphere of prayer by asking someone to light the prayer candle. Call the group to prayer with these words:

   Let us remember God's presence here among us today as we begin our prayer in the name of the Father, and of the Son, and of the Holy Spirit. Amen.

3. Share the following reflection:

   God, too often we label people. We look at the way someone dresses or wears their hair, without taking the time to get to know anything about the real person. All we see is the outside shell. We make fun of people, and sometimes we even start fights. Why? Just because some people are different from us? Everybody is different in their own way, but some people just show it more than others. God, help us to realize that people's differences are something to enjoy, not criticize. What a boring world it would be if everybody were exactly the same. (Carl Koch, *Dreams Alive*, p. 56)

4. Conclude with this prayer. Ask the young people to repeat each line after you.

   Starting today, Lord, give us courage to be ourselves.

   Starting today, Lord, help us work together as a team.

   Starting today, Lord, help us put you at the center of all we do.

   Starting today, Lord, help us live as a people created in your own image.

Sticking Together (9:10 A.M.)

1. Ask the retreatants to find the other members of their group by joining those who have the same color sticker on their name tags. Each group can sit in a circle on the floor somewhere in the meeting space. Share with retreatants that these are their small groups for the retreat day.

Hot Potato (9:15 A.M.)

Preparation

- Gather the following supplies:
  - ❑ small square beanbags, one for each small group
  - ❑ a CD player
  - ❑ one or more lively Christian rock CDs

1. Introduce this activity in the following way:

   This activity is called "Hot Potato." I will give you a beanbag, which will be the hot potato. When the music starts, please pass the hot potato around your circle. As long as the music is playing, you continue passing the hot potato.

> When the music stops, the person holding the hot potato must stand up. He or she will then receive a challenge. From then on until the game is over, when that person receives the hot potato, he or she must stand up and perform the challenge.
>
> Challenges never go away. And you can have more than one. Any questions?

2. Start the music and let it play as the hot potato goes around each group at least twice during the first round. Stop the music and award the challenge. For example, "Moo like a cow" means that the person must stand up and moo like a cow whenever he or she gets the hot potato.

   Continue the game, varying the length of time the music plays and the challenges that are assigned. Here are some possible options. Feel free to make up your own too, but be sure that none of the challenges are hurtful or demeaning.

   - sing the ABC song
   - stand on one foot and hop up and down
   - pat your head and rub your tummy at the same time
   - crow like a rooster

3. End the game by thanking all for being good sports. Stress the need to have fun and play together when people are getting to know one another for the first time.

The Color of Diversity (9:45 A.M.)

Preparation

- Gather the following supplies:
  - ❑ copies of handout 4, "Rainbow Outline," on legal-size paper, one for each small group
  - ❑ small plastic bags, one for each small group
  - ❑ packs of crayons of only one color, one pack each for half of the small groups
  - ❑ packs of multicolored crayons, one pack each for half of the small groups
- Sort the crayons and put them into small plastic bags so half of the groups have crayons of only one color and the other half have crayons of the traditional mixture of colors. For example, if you have ten groups, five get bags of crayons of only one color and five get bags of multicolored crayons.

1. Introduce this activity in the following way:

> We will begin today's session with an art task. In a few minutes, I will give each small group a picture and some crayons.
>
> Your group's job is to make the most colorful, creative picture. You want yours to be completely different from everyone else's. You must all work together as a group to complete this picture. One person cannot do all the work.
>
> You may want to come up with a plan before you even pick up a crayon. You will have only 7 minutes to create your picture.

2. Give each small group a copy of the handout. Give half the groups bags of single-colored crayons. Give the other groups bags of multicolored crayons. Direct the groups to begin their work. Be sure to call time checks at the 5-minute and 3-minute marks. Have each small group share its picture with the large group.

3. Ask retreatants to share their answers to these questions:
   - Was it a challenge for some groups to have crayons of only one color?
   - What does this say about diversity?
   - How can you connect this activity to experiences in your own life?

   Some possible answers:
   - It is harder to be creative and colorful when you have crayons of only one color.
   - Life would be boring if everything were the same.
   - Relationships would be boring if everyone were the same.
   - Diversity is a blessing that enriches our lives. For example, it is great to have different kinds of friends and different levels of friendships. Different friends share different interests. Different friends are good for sharing different problems.
   - If everyone knew the same things and came from the same place and had the same experiences, there would be nothing we could learn from one another.

4. Close by summarizing the retreatants' answers and emphasizing the need for and value of diversity in our world and in each of our lives.

If We Could All Be the Same (10:10 A.M.)

Preparation

- Gather the following supplies:
  - ❑ newsprint
  - ❑ markers

1. Ask retreatants to list some of the differences they encounter in different people. Fill a sheet of newsprint with their ideas, such as race, gender, age, disabilities, nationality, economic status, and geographic boundaries.

2. Offer the following directions:

   For 10 minutes, and only the next 10 minutes, your small groups have a special power. You have the power to change the world so there are no longer any of the differences we have listed to divide us. If you give the word, there will no longer be differences in skin color, people will all have the same amount of money, and all disabilities will be gone.

   Would you do it?

Take some time to talk about it in your groups. Be prepared to defend your position by answering one of the following questions:

Why would you make the change?

Why would you not do anything?

3. When 10 minutes have passed, ask each small group to choose a spokesperson to share the group's answers and reasons with the large group. Invite each spokesperson to come forward, and challenge each to explain and defend his or her answers. Ask other groups to honor and respect the responses even if they disagree with them.

What Color Is God? (10:35 A.M.)

Preparation

- Gather the following supplies:
  - ❑ small bags of M&M's, one bag for each person

1. Ask the retreatants to take a blank sheet of paper from their journals or the supply basket on their table. Introduce the activity with these or similar words:

   I am going to give you a word. When you hear this word, I want you to think of a color and write the color on your piece of paper. Do not tell anyone what you wrote on the paper until I direct you to do so.

   The word is *God*!

2. After everyone has written down a color, engage the large group in a discussion about what they wrote and their reasons for choosing the colors they did. Ask:

- What color did you choose to describe God? Why?
- Comment on the variety of colors chosen and the variety of reasons given for the same color.

Continue the large-group discussion with the following questions:

- Based on your answers, what can we learn about God?
- What can we learn about our relationship with God?
- What do you think God sees when God looks at each one of us?
- What are your thoughts about being created in the image and likeness of God?

3. Ask one last question: When I think about how God created us, I think of M&M's. Can anyone guess why?

   After the retreatants have responded, affirm their answers and summarize them with these or similar words:

   We have learned from an early age that we are created in the image and likeness of God. Just as we are all different from one another in many ways, on the inside and the outside, we all differ in our views of God, our ways of describing God, and our ways of approaching God.

> M&M's are different on the inside and the outside. They have different colors on the outside. They are different on the inside, too, because some have nutty or crunchy centers. They come in different size bags and containers.
>
> Yet all M&M's have chocolate in common. In the same way, even though we are all different, we are all created in God's image and we are all loved tremendously by God.

Close this activity by summarizing the answers of the retreatants and rewarding the efforts of all with small bags of M&M's to enjoy during their break.

Break (11:00 A.M.)

Video Challenges (11:20 A.M.)

Preparation

- Gather the following supplies:
  - ❏ a large-screen TV
  - ❏ a VCR or DVD player
  - ❏ movie tapes or DVDs (see below)
- Identify scenes from movies—fairly recent ones, if possible—that highlight issues of diversity. They can be positive or negative issues. You should have at least two scenes that are 3 to 6 minutes long. Cue the tapes to the scenes before the retreat. These are some possibilities:
  - *The Mask* (1994, New Line Entertainment, 101 minutes, rated PG-13); differences in appearance
  - *Save the Last Dance* (2001, Paramount Home Video, 113 minutes, rated PG-13); racial and economic diversity
  - *Spider Man* (2002, Columbia-TriStar, 121 minutes, rated PG-13); people who are teased for being "brains"

1. Show the movie scenes you have chosen. Then ask the group to discuss the following questions. Be prepared to revise some of these questions based on the videos you choose.

- What type of diversity is highlighted in these clips?
- What challenges do the characters face?
- Share examples of this diversity issue found in our everyday world.

2. Finish by discussing these general questions together:

- Is there enough diversity in the movies? in other types of media?
- How does Hollywood affect our response to people who are different from us?

Lunch (12:00 P.M.)

Clue Hunt (12:30 P.M.)

Preparation

- Gather the following supplies:
  - ❑ copies of handout 5, "Clue Hunt Directions," one for each small group
  - ❑ copies of handout 6, "Diversity Within Unity," one for each small group
  - ❑ large index cards
- Write the following words and phrases on the index cards, one word or phrase per card:
  - Body of Christ
  - unique
  - gifts and talents
  - service
  - gifts
  - calls
  - celebrate
  - community
- Choose a site for your clue hunt. It would be best to go outside, if possible. If the outdoor grounds are not large, you can hide clues both inside and outside. Hide the index cards with the words or phrases in different locations when the retreatants will not see what you are doing.

1. Give each small group a copy of handout 5 and review it with them. Then send the groups out to search.

2. When each small group returns, distribute handout 6. Ask the groups to fill in the blanks on the handout using the words and phrases they found. If they do it correctly, they will create a reflection on diversity within unity. When all the groups have had a chance to complete the reflection sheet, have someone read it to the whole group. Affirm the groups for working together on this task, and stress the importance of using a diversity of gifts and talents in building the Reign of God.

Alternative Activity: You can make this activity easier or harder by adding clues specific to your locality. For example, if the parish grounds or retreat center you are visiting has an outdoor stations of the cross, one of the clues can be: "Read John 19:15–16. This Scripture explains the beginning of the stations of the cross. Travel to this area to find your word."

Break (1:15 P.M.)

What Would Jesus Do? (1:30 P.M.)

Preparation

- Gather the following supplies:
  - ❑ index cards, one for each small group

1. Distribute an index card to each small group. Introduce this activity in the following way:

   Earlier we talked about how strange the world would be if we all were the same and how our wonderful, wise God loves variety. We used movie clips to help discuss some tough issues in this world.

   Now we will take some time to look at tough situations you encounter in your own lives. Please think of a situation—at school, with friends, in your family—when someone just was not treated right. It could be a time when someone left you out or when you excluded others. It can be an example of how people were mistreated or misjudged because of the color of their skin, or the school they attend, or the team they play for, or the way they dress. Decide on one situation for your small group.

   Please write two or three sentences describing the situation on your index card.

2. After 5 minutes, collect all the index cards and glance at them briefly to make sure each small group followed directions. Scramble the cards and redistribute them to the groups, making sure no group gets its original card. Ask each group to read the situation on its card and prepare a response to present to the whole group. Here are two possible options for responses:

   - Option 1: Prepare and present a role-play of what Jesus would do in the situation.
   - Option 2: Describe the situation and what the group thinks Jesus would do in the situation.

   Allow about 10 minutes for the groups to work on the task. Then invite each group to share its presentation.

3. Conclude the activity by encouraging retreatants to invite Jesus into a situation when they are not quite sure how to handle it. We must all allow the example of Jesus to guide us in how we treat others who are different from ourselves.

Prayer Patch Tapestry (2:00 P.M.)

Preparation

- Gather the following supplies:
  - ❑ 5-by-5-inch squares of multicolored construction paper, one for each retreatant
  - ❑ 4.5-by-4.5-inch squares of white paper, one for each retreatant
  - ❑ glue or glue sticks
  - ❑ a pack of multicultural crayons for each group (yes, there actually are multicultural crayons, made by Crayola)
  - ❑ newsprint
  - ❑ markers

- Glue the squares of white paper onto the squares of multicolored paper so that there is a multicolored border around each white square. The squares are now prayer patches.

1. Give each person a prayer patch. Have each recap the day by asking, "What are some of the things you learned from the retreat sessions today?" As they share their answers, record them on the newsprint. When they are done answering, post the newsprint where everyone in the group can see it.

2. Divide the large group into pairs. Ask the partners to talk with each other and choose a word or phrase from the flip chart. Then they should think of one or more symbols together to represent the word or phrase, and draw the symbols on their prayer patches. For example, a pair could illustrate the phrase "working together" with stick figures holding hands or the "gift of diversity" with a rainbow-colored hand. They can use several symbols together to create a patch, but they should avoid using words. Let them know that the prayer patches will make up a tapestry that will be used during the closing prayer. If time permits, invite retreatants to share their symbols in foursomes.

Note: If you have a very large group, you may ask each pair to create one patch. If your group is small, each person can make his or her own patch.

Come, All You People (2:30 P.M.)

Preparation

- Gather the following supplies:
  - ❑ a CD player
  - ❑ two or three candles
  - ❑ music for opening and closing songs
  - ❑ an easel and a piece of poster board large enough to be the backing for all the tapestry squares when they are put together
  - ❑ masking tape
  - ❑ prayer squares (from previous activity)
  - ❑ copies of handout 7, "American Indian Prayer," one for each retreatant
- Choose a song for the tapestry procession. Try to choose one that focuses on diversity.
- Choose gathering and closing songs for the prayer service that are bilingual or multicultural. "Come, All You People/*Uyai Mose*" by Alexander Gondo (*Gather Comprehensive*, GIA Publications) and "I Say Yes, My Lord" by Donna Pena (*Gather Comprehensive*, GIA Publications) are recommended and are found in many popular hymnals.
- Recruit a young person to proclaim Galatians 3:26–29.

1. Prepare the prayer space. Place the blank poster board on an easel near the front of the space. Teach the opening and closing songs to the group. When you are through practicing, distribute the copies of handout 7 and light the candles to signal the beginning of prayer.

2. Begin by inviting everyone to join you in singing the gathering song. Then offer the following prayer:

    Today, we have celebrated our differences and discovered that there can be unity in diversity. As we close the retreat, let us bring our prayers to the God who created us in his image and loves us in all our wonderful variety. Let us pray for one another and remember always that we are all one in Jesus Christ.

3. Invite the person who has prepared the reading to come forward and proclaim the Scripture passage. Allow a few moments of silence following the reading.

4. Invite the retreatants to come forward two at a time to tape their prayer patches on the poster board. Ask them to do this slowly and reverently, noting that the covered poster board will become a diversity tapestry. During this time, play the song you have chosen for the tapestry procession.

5. Introduce the sign of peace by talking about how Jesus reached out to all people in peace and how we offer this sign today—just as we do every time we gather for the Eucharist—as a sign of our willingness to share the peace of Christ with all other people, regardless of our differences.

6. Invite the whole group to pray aloud the "American Indian Prayer" on handout 7. You may wish to consider dividing the group into "left" and "right" sections that take turns reading sentences.

7. Invite the retreat leaders to go out into the community of retreatants and offer a blessing or commission. The retreatants can also be invited to bless one another. The gesture should be one that is comfortable for young people, such as a hug, special handshake, sign of the cross on the hand, and so on. The gesture is a challenge to take what they have learned at the retreat and put it into action.

8. Offer the following prayer:

    We are all members of the Body of Christ.
    Each of us is unique, created in God's image.
    Each of us has special gifts and talents that God calls us to use to serve others.
    Through the Holy Spirit, God calls each of us to live our lives as Jesus would.
    We recognize and understand that our diversity and uniqueness are gifts to the world.
    Amen.

9. Conclude by singing the closing song you have selected.

Alternative Ideas for This Retreat

Here are some activity ideas that can be used for a longer version of this retreat or as alternative activities.

- Compare and contrast music that divides with music that unites. There are many examples of both in contemporary music.
- How did Jesus react to people who were different from him? Locate examples in the Scriptures. Find parallels to life today.
- Write a “Creed of Acceptance” that states how you, as a group, will treat others.
- Contact your local Catholic Social Agency branch and see if someone can lead a follow-up session on conflict resolution skills.

Handout 3

Me Too

Complete each statement with a word or phrase that is true of you. When you are finished, look for people with similar answers. When you find someone with a matching answer, sign each other's sheets on the blank line to the left of the matching statements.

__________ 1. My favorite sport to play is ____________________

__________ 2. My favorite music group is ____________________

__________ 3. A place I would like to visit some day is ____________________

__________ 4. My favorite television show is ____________________

__________ 5. My favorite color of M&M's candy is ____________________

__________ 6. A chore I absolutely hate doing is ____________________

__________ 7. The job I would least like to have is ____________________

__________ 8. When I am under stress, I usually ____________________

__________ 9. When I was five, my favorite story was ____________________

__________ 10. My favorite comic strip or cartoon character is ____________________

__________ 11. A well-known person I admire is ____________________

__________ 12. My favorite fast-food restaurant is ____________________

__________ 13. My favorite flavor of ice cream is ____________________

__________ 14. If I could be famous, I would like to be known for ____________________

__________ 15. My favorite breakfast cereal is ____________________

(Adapted from Marilyn Kielbasa, *Community Building Ideas for Ministry with Young Teens* [Winona, MN: Saint Mary's Press, 2001], pages 54–55. Copyright © 2001 by Saint Mary's Press. All rights reserved.)

Handout 4

Rainbow Outline

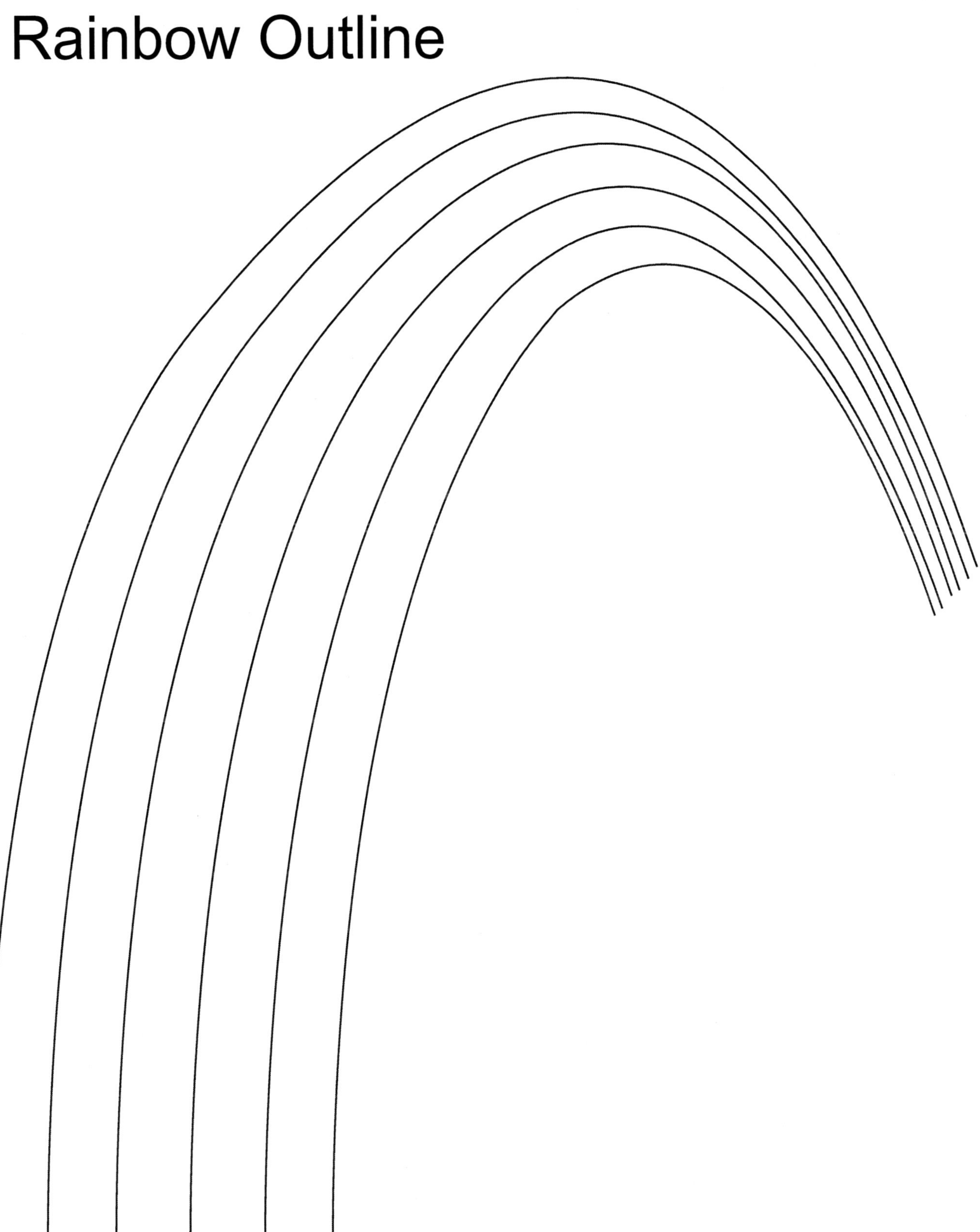

Handout 5

Clue Hunt Directions

Your goal is to find eight cards with words or phrases written on them that are hidden in different places on the parish or retreat center grounds. Each card is hidden in a different place. Please use the following guidelines:

1. You must travel as a group and work as a group.
2. Each time you find a word or phrase, write it down on the back of this piece of paper.
3. Your group may not communicate with any other group during this activity.
4. Be respectful of the environment, the property, and other visitors.
5. If you have any questions, ask the adult who is traveling with you. He or she is not permitted to give you the location of the words.
6. DO NOT REMOVE THE WORDS OR PHRASES FROM THE PLACES YOU VISIT.
7. After your group finds all eight words or phrases, return to the starting point, where you will be given one final task to complete.

Handout 6

Diversity Within Unity

We are all members of the ______________________. Each of us is ______________________, created in God's image. Each of us has special ______________________ and ______________________, which God calls us to place at the ______________________ of the Church and others. Through the ______________________ of the Holy Spirit, God ______________________ each of us to live our lives as Jesus would. We recognize and ______________________ that our diversity and uniqueness are gifts to the ______________________.

Handout 7

American Indian Prayer

O Great Spirit,
Whose voice I hear in the winds,
And whose breath gives life to all the world, hear me! I am small
and weak.
I need your strength and wisdom.
Let me walk in beauty, and make my eyes ever behold the red
and purple sunset.
Make my hands respect the things you have made and my ears
sharp to hear your voice.
Make me wise so that I may understand things you have taught
my people.
Let me learn the lessons you have hidden in every leaf and rock.
I seek strength, not to be greater than my brother but to fight my
greatest enemy—myself.
Make me always ready to come to you with clean hands
and straight eyes.
So when life fades, as the fading sunset, my spirit may come to
you without shame.

(Taken from *A Book of Prayers* [Dubuque, IA: Harcourt Religion Publishers, 1990], page 28. Copyright © 1990 by Harcourt Religion Publishers. Used with permission.)

-Retreat 3

It's a Miracle

Introduction

"It's a Miracle" is an overnight retreat that invites young people to explore the miracles of Jesus and his power to transform our lives.

Goals

- To assist the retreatants in recognizing and celebrating each person as a miracle of God's creation.
- To help retreatants discover the miraculous healing touch of Jesus in our everyday lives.
- To offer opportunities for them to experience the wonder and awe of God in the amazing miracles of Jesus and to grow in faith as they experience the power of God.
- To help retreatants experience Jesus, the miracle worker, who changed the lives of all he met, and to allow God to transform lives.

Schedule

The following sequence for "It's a Miracle" is just one suggestion on how to arrange the schedule. Use the column labeled "Actual Plan" to record the activities, sequences, and starting times that will work for you.

Time	*Activity Name*	*Activity Type*	*Actual Plan*
Friday evening			
6:30 P.M.	Arrival		________
6:50 P.M.	Welcome and Opening Talk	Theme talk	________
7:10 P.M.	The Lifesaver Games	Icebreaker	________
7:40 P.M.	Miracle Groups	Small-group formation	________
7:45 P.M.	In Search of a Miracle	Scripture activity	________
8:20 P.M.	Snack Break		________
8:40 P.M.	Jesus and the Blind Man	Scripture proclamation	________
9:00 P.M.	Take Off the Blindfolds	Discussion	________
9:45 P.M.	Break		________
10:00 P.M.	The Boy Cured of a Demon	Witness talk	________
10:20 P.M.	Pray It! Study It! Live It!	Discussion	________
11:00 P.M.	Prayer to Cast Out Demons	Night prayer	________
12:00 A.M.	Lights Out		________
Saturday			
7:45 A.M.	Rising		________
8:30 A.M.	Breakfast		________
9:00 A.M.	Fishbowl	Icebreaker	________
9:30 A.M.	The Loaves and Fish	Witness talk	________
9:50 A.M.	Blessing Bread, Breaking Bread, Sharing Bread	Preparing prayer	________
10:30 A.M.	Prayer		________
11:00 A.M.	Break		________
11:30 A.M.	The Wedding Feast at Cana	Scripture proclamation	________
11:40 A.M.	Water Relay Race	Icebreaker	________
12:00 P.M.	Questions in Clay Pots	Discussion	________
12:30 P.M.	Lunch		________
1:15 P.M.	Jesus Raises Lazarus from the Dead	Scripture proclamation	________
1:30 P.M.	Speechless	Video, music Quiet, journaling	________

2:30 P.M.	Break		________
3:00 P.M.	Jesus Calms the Storm	Witness talk	________
3:20 P.M.	Islands of Safety	Activity	________
4:30 P.M.	Closing Liturgy		________
5:30 P.M.	Dinner		________

General Materials and Preparation

- The suggested space needs for this retreat include a large gathering space, tables for small groups, and a designated prayer space.
- Gather the following items:
  - ❑ name tags, one for each retreatant
  - ❑ journals, one for each person
- Before the retreat, assign retreatants to small groups of approximately eight people. Assign one teen team member and one adult team member to each group.
- Assign each group the name of a miracle that will be used during the retreat: Jesus and the Blind Man, The Boy Cured of a Demon, The Loaves and Fish, The Wedding Feast at Cana, Jesus Raises Lazarus from the Dead, or Jesus Calms the Storm. Write each person's name on the inside front cover of a journal and the name of the miracle group they are assigned to on the inside back cover.
- Create a portable supply basket for each small group, containing the following frequently used items:
  - ❑ pens or pencils
  - ❑ markers
  - ❑ scissors
  - ❑ glue sticks
  - ❑ self-stick notes
  - ❑ songbooks or hymnals
  - ❑ copies of *The Catholic Youth Bible* or another Bible
- Place a basket at each group table.

Detailed Description of Activities for Friday

Welcome and Opening Talk (6:50 P.M.)

Preparation

- Ask a team member to prepare a 20-minute opening talk to introduce the theme of the retreat. To help the person prepare, give her or him a copy of resource 3, "Suggestions for Welcome and Opening Talk," as well as a copy of appendix A, "Helpful Hints for Giving Talks."

1. When all the retreatants have arrived, welcome everyone and introduce the retreat team. Then introduce the person giving the welcome talk. After she or he is finished, review the retreat ground rules and make any needed announcements.

The Life Saver Games (7:10 P.M.)

Preparation

- Gather the following supplies:
  - ❑ individually wrapped Life Savers, one bag for each small group of eight
  - ❑ newsprint, two sheets for each group
  - ❑ markers, one pack for each group

Life Saver Traveling Relay

1. Divide the large group into small groups of eight. Divide the groups again so four team members are on one side of the room and four are facing them on the other side of the room. Provide each team with one Life Saver.

2. Tell the retreatants that the goal of this game is to travel with the Life Saver from one end of the room to the other without using their hands or arms. Also, they may not use their hands when passing the Life Saver to the next person in the relay. They may, for example, blow the Life Saver across the floor or carry it on top of a foot. The team who completes the task first wins!

Wordy Life Savers

1. Give each group a bag of Life Savers, a sheet of newsprint, and markers.

2. Tell the groups that their task is to spell words using the Life Savers. The words must have something to do with faith or the retreat theme, for example, the word *pray*. The adult team member will record on newsprint each word they create.

3. After 10 minutes of Life Saver spelling, post the lists of words on the walls of the retreat space.

Twenty Uses for a Life Saver

1. Ask retreatants to remain in the same groups for the next challenge. Ask them to spend 5 minutes to come up with twenty different creative uses for a Life Saver. They may not include the obvious one, eating a Life Saver, or any of the ways Life Savers were used in previous games during the evening. Invite the adult in each group to jot down each of the ideas. Allow about 10 minutes for this task. Then invite each group to present a few of its ideas to the entire group.

2. After all the Life Saver games are over, ask retreatants to identify what they have learned from these events. They will likely list skills such as communication, teamwork, creativity, patience, persistence, imagination, and problem solving. Encourage them to make good use of these skills throughout the retreat.

Miracle Groups (7:40 P.M.)

Preparation

- Gather the following supplies:
  - ❑ retreatants' journals

1. Distribute a journal to each person. Ask people to look inside the back cover. Direct the retreatants to find the people who have the same miracle retreat theme inside the back cover of their journals. When the retreatants have formed groups, direct each group to find a table and sit down together. Invite them to introduce themselves to the other members of their new groups. Tell them that this will be their small group for all retreat activities and discussions.

2. Now offer some comments about the use of journaling during the retreat:

   Journaling helps us get in touch with our feelings. Sometimes writing something down is easier than talking about it.

   Because journaling can be a powerful way to get in touch with our feelings and communicate with God, during the retreat you will be asked to use a journal to write down reactions to talks and activities.

   Please bring your journals to every activity during the retreat and plan to write in them often.

In Search of a Miracle (7:45 P.M.)

1. Introduce this activity in these or similar words:

   We have a lot of great activities, talks, and prayers planned for you during this retreat. As we heard in the opening talk, our retreat theme centers on the miracles of Jesus. During this activity, you will be working together as a team to search the Gospels for examples of the miracles of Jesus. By working together and sharing what we learn from the Scriptures, we begin to explore the miracles of Jesus and how they connect with our own lives.

1. Ask the participants to take a Bible from their supply basket. Tell them to find various examples of the miracles Jesus performed in the bibles. You may wish to note that all such examples are found in the four Gospels. Note that as they find examples, they should record the miracle and the citation in which it is described on a blank sheet of paper. Challenge each person to find at least a dozen examples. Once each person has completed this task, ask the group members to compare their lists and discuss each miracle identified.

2. Invite the groups to offer some examples of the miracles they found. You may even wish to note some of the miracles not mentioned. Thank the retreatants for sharing in groups and encourage them to participate actively in all retreat activities. Close this activity by letting participants know that during the retreat they will be exploring a few of the miracles they identified in greater depth.

Snack Break (8:20 P.M.)

Jesus and the Blind Man (8:40 P.M.)

Preparation

- Gather the following supplies:
  - ❑ copies of handout 8, "Jesus and the Blind Man: Luke 18:35–43," one for each retreatant
- Assign readers to take on the four roles found on the handout. Ask the readers to rehearse the choral reading beforehand.

1. Provide each participant with a copy of handout 8. Introduce this activity in the following way:

   We began the retreat with some icebreaker games to get to know one another. We have formed groups and started to name many of the miracles of Jesus found in the Scriptures. For the next several activities, we will focus on one miracle, Jesus's healing the blind man. As we begin, we invite you to join in proclaiming the Scripture passage, Luke 18:35–43.

2. Conduct the reading as noted on handout 8.

3. Allow 10 minutes of quiet time for retreatants to reflect on the Scripture passage and to write in their journals. Some questions they might consider include these:

- Why do you think Jesus performed this miracle?
- How can you relate this miracle to your everyday life?

Take Off the Blindfolds (9:00 P.M.)

Preparation

- Gather the following supplies:
  - ❑ bandanas, one for each retreatant. Choose a different color for each group. As an alternative, you can use strips of scrap material.
  - ❑ copies of resource 4, "Take Off the Blindfolds," one for each small group
  - ❑ small safety pins, one for each participant
- Cut apart questions from resource 4 and pin one question to each bandana. You should have a complete set for each group.

Note: Some young people may not be comfortable with being blindfolded. Allow some to just observe this activity if they prefer. Also, be sure there is adequate adult supervision.

1. Provide group leaders with a blindfold for each group member. Invite leaders to move through the group and blindfold their group members.

2. Ask retreatants, one group at a time, to move slowly and carefully to another part of the room. Remind everyone of the need to follow directions and be serious about this task, so as to avoid injury.

3. As the groups arrive at the new location, ask participants to take off their blindfolds and begin discussing the questions that have been pinned to the blindfolds. Each person should read his or her question, answer the question, and then invite each group member to answer as well. Note that each group member should have an opportunity to answer before the next person addresses his or her question.

4. Close the activity by affirming retreatants and encouraging them to continue a good spirit of discussion throughout the retreat. Ask them to wear their bandanas for the rest of the retreat as a reminder to be open to God's miracles working in their lives. (*Note*: They can wear a bandana through a belt loop of their jeans, on their head or arm, around their neck, or even attached to their prayer journal.)

Break (9:45 P.M.)

The Boy Cured of a Demon (10:00 P.M.)

Preparation

- Ask a team member to prepare a 15-minute talk on the Boy Cured of a Demon. To help the person prepare, give him or her a copy of resource 5, "Suggestions for the Boy Cured of a Demon Talk," as well as a copy of appendix A, "Helpful Hints for Giving Talks."

1. Introduce the team member giving this talk.

2. After the talk, allow 5 minutes for quiet reflection and journal writing.

Pray It! Study It! Live It! (10:20 P.M.)

Preparation

- Gather the following supplies:
  - ❏ copies of handout 9, "Pray It! Study It! Live It!" one for each person
  - ❏ newsprint
  - ❏ markers

1. Distribute the copies of handout 9 and provide each group with a sheet of newsprint and a marker. Ask everyone to work quietly on their own for 10 minutes to read the miracle Scripture Mark 9:14–19 and then write their answers to the questions on the handout.

2. Invite the retreatants to share their answers in their small groups. Choose one person in each group to record the key points on the sheet of newsprint provided. Allow about 15 minutes for discussion.

3. Invite a spokesperson from each group to summarize the work of the group and share it with the larger group. You may wish to post the newsprint lists on the wall.

4. Close by emphasizing the importance of not only reading or hearing the word proclaimed but of reflecting on the word of God and breaking open the word of God with others. Suggest that the Pray It! Study It! Live It! model is an approach they can adopt and use after this retreat experience.

Prayer to Cast Out Demons (11:00 P.M.)

Preparation

- Gather the following supplies:
  - ❑ a votive candle, candleholder, and matches for each group
  - ❑ four copies of resource 6, "Prayer to Cast Out Demons: Mark 9:14–29"
  - ❑ one large candle
- Assign the Scripture reading as found in resource 6 to four people. Be sure they practice the reading prior to the beginning of the prayer service.

1. Invite the retreatants to join you in the prayer space. Ask them to be seated with their small groups. Provide each group with a candle and matches. Allow a minute or two for everyone to get settled.

2. Begin the prayer by lighting the large candle and placing it at the front (or in the middle) of the room. Then invite everyone to make the sign of the cross.

3. Now invite the four assigned readers to stand and proclaim the Scripture as found on resource 6. Allow a few minutes of silence following the reading.

4. Invite one person from each small group to light the candle the group has been given. Then ask that the candle be passed slowly around the group. Each person should complete the following prayer before passing the candle on to the next person:

   Lord, please cast out the demon of . . .

   Let the retreatants know they can complete the prayer aloud or silently. Allow enough time for all groups to complete this prayer action.

5. Now invite the retreatants to pass the candle around each small group again. This time ask each person to pray the following prayer before passing the candle on to the next person:

   Lord, help my unbelief.

   Again, let the retreatants know they can complete the prayer aloud or silently. Allow enough time for all groups to complete this prayer action.

6. To conclude the activity, invite the retreatants to join hands and pray the Lord's Prayer together. Close with the sign of the cross. Then ask the retreatants to leave the prayer space quietly.

(This prayer service is adapted from Maryann Hakowski, *22 Ready-Made Prayer Services with 100 Extra Prayer Ideas*, pp. 106–107.)

Lights Out (12:00 A.M.)

Detailed Description of Activities for Saturday

Rising (7:45 A.M.)

Breakfast (8:30 A.M.)

Fishbowl (9:00 A.M.)

Preparation

- Gather the following supplies:
  - ❏ one large fishbowl (or a large, clear bowl)
  - ❏ one copy of resource 7, "Fishbowl Questions"
- Arrange chairs in two rows, with the chairs facing each other. For a large group, several sets of chairs may be needed. Every retreatant will need a chair.
- Cut apart the questions on resource 7 and mix them up in the fishbowl.

1. Welcome everyone back, and conduct a brief review of last evening's activities. Then introduce this activity in the following way:

> This activity gives us an opportunity to renew our discussion from last night and get us thinking again about the topic of the retreat, the miracles of Jesus. In this fishbowl are questions about miracles. I will ask one volunteer at a time to pick a question and read it to the entire group. Some cards contain questions; others ask you to complete a sentence. Take a minute to think about the question or sentence, and then give your answer only to the person sitting across from you. Make sure you provide a brief explanation of your answer. You will have a different partner for each question.

2. Tell one of the rows that it will be the "moveable row," that is, at the end of each turn, the first person in that row will get up and walk to the end of the row. Everyone else in the row will shift down one chair. Begin by inviting someone to come forward and choose a question. Then allow time for the retreatants to share their answers. Continue in this fashion until all the questions have been asked or the allotted time has been used. Make sure that after each question, when everyone is finished discussing it, the people in the "moveable row" switch chairs.

(This activity is adapted from Maryann Hakowski, *Growing with Jesus*, pp. 147–148.)

The Loaves and Fish (9:30 A.M.)

Preparation

- Ask a team member to prepare a 15-minute talk on the Loaves and Fish. To help the person prepare, give him or her a copy of resource 8, "Suggestions for the Loaves and Fish Talk," as well as a copy of appendix A, "Helpful Hints for Giving Talks."

1. Introduce the team member giving this talk.

2. After the talk, allow 5 minutes for quiet reflection and journal writing.

Blessing Bread, Breaking Bread, Sharing Bread (9: 50 A.M.)

Preparation

- Gather the following supplies:
  - ❑ three copies of handout 10, "Blessing Bread, Breaking Bread, Sharing Bread"
- Designate three separate rooms or spaces where three groups can work without interrupting one another.

1. Divide participants into three groups. Give each group one copy of handout 10. Then introduce this activity in the following way:

> This morning, you all have the opportunity to participate in creating our morning prayer. Bread is the center of our prayer. Each group will plan a portion of a prayer experience. Using the handout provided, you will have about 40 minutes to conduct your planning. Read the instructions noted on the handout and complete the task assigned to your group—either blessing bread, breaking bread, or sharing bread.

2. Gather the groups together again and have each conduct its assigned portion of prayer. Affirm the good work and creativity shown by each group. Acknowledge that prayer takes patience and work—whether we pray as individuals or as a group.

Break (11:00 A.M.)

The Wedding Feast at Cana (11:30 A.M.)

Preparation

- Gather the following supplies:
  - ❏ four copies of resource 9, “The Wedding Feast at Cana”
- Assign the Scripture reading as found in resource 9 to four people. Be sure they practice the reading.

1. Introduce this activity in the following way:

> Last night we began with an overview of the miracles of Jesus and then spent some time looking closely at the stories of the Blind Man and the Boy Cured of a Demon. We began this morning with the story of the Loaves and Fish. Now we will spend some time focusing on the story of the Wedding Feast at Cana.

2. Invite the first reader to begin the proclamation of the reading and continue as noted on the resource. When the reading is concluded, allow a moment of silence.

3. Invite the retreatants to spend some quiet time reflecting on the Scripture passage and writing in their journals. Allow about 10 minutes for this task.

Water Relay Race (11:40 A.M.)

Preparation

- Gather the following supplies for each group:
  - ❏ a clear, empty one-gallon wine bottle
  - ❏ a packet of powdered grape drink
  - ❏ a large pot of water
  - ❏ a soup ladle
- Rinse the wine bottles out and allow them to dry completely. Pour one packet of the powdered grape drink into each dry wine bottle. Fill the pots with water.
- Line up the water pots and ladles at one end of a large room. Line up the wine bottles at the other end of the room. If weather permits, you may want to hold this activity outside; if not, you will want to protect the flooring in the meeting space by putting down newspaper or plastic.

1. Ask the members of each group to line up behind a water pot. Tell them that at your signal, they will begin a relay race. Using only a ladle, they must transfer the water from the pot to the wine bottle. Ask them to take notice of what happens to the water during the relay race. Cheer on the teams, and congratulate the winners.

Questions in Clay Pots (12:00 P.M.)

Preparation

- Gather the following supplies:
  - ❑ medium-sized clay pots, one for each small group
  - ❑ one set of discussion questions from resource 10, "Questions in Clay Pots," for each group
- Cut apart the questions from resource 10 and place one set in each of the clay pots.

1. Provide each group with a clay pot with the question strips inside it. Invite the groups to begin answering the questions. Each person should choose a question, read it aloud, and answer it. The person should then invite others in the group to answer as well. Allow about 20 minutes for the group discussions.

2. Conclude by noting the following:

   The Wedding Feast at Cana is often considered to be the first miracle of Jesus. We can learn a lot about relationships by watching how Jesus responds to his mother and to the wedding couple in need. Also, his miracles took place around events in ordinary lives, and he used ordinary elements, such as water and wine, to allow the power and love of God to be expressed through him. Let us, too, be open to the ways in which Jesus can transform our lives and the lives of others.

Lunch (12:30 P.M.)

Jesus Raises Lazarus from the Dead (1:15 P.M.)

Preparation

- Gather the following supplies:
  - ❑ copies of handout 11, "Jesus Raises Lazarus from the Dead: John 11:1–44," one for each retreatant
- Assign the Scripture reading as found on handout 11 to four people. Be sure they practice the reading.

1. Provide each person with a copy of handout 11. Then introduce this portion of the retreat in the following way:

   This morning we explored the miracle of the Loaves and Fish and reflected on the Wedding Feast at Cana. For the next two activities, we will focus on the miracle of Jesus's raising Lazarus from the dead. As we begin, we invite you to join in proclaiming the Scripture from the Gospel of John 11:1–44.

2. Invite the first assigned reader to begin the proclamation. Continue as instructed on the handout.

3. Invite the retreatants to reflect on the Scripture passage and write in their journals. Allow about 10 minutes for this task.

Speechless (1:30 P.M.)

Preparation

- Gather the following supplies:
  - ❑ a CD player and a CD recording of "Speechless" from the collection titled *Speechless*, by Stephen Curtis Chapman (Sparrow Records, 1999), or the video or DVD clip of "The Raising of Lazarus" from *Jesus of Nazareth* (RAI/ITC Entertainment LTD, 1993, 382 minutes, not rated)
- Cue up the CD or DVD player or VCR and make sure your equipment is working properly.

1. Introduce this activity in the following way:

> Sometimes our lives get so busy and frantic. There is so much to do, so many places to go, so much homework to finish. Sometimes our lives are filled with nonstop noise and interruptions. There are cell phones ringing and computer games to play. The radio is on, the iPod is playing, the TV is blaring. No wonder it is hard to find the space and the quiet to spend some time talking to God. In a few moments, you will hear a song (or watch a video clip). Listen carefully to the response to Jesus's raising Lazarus from the dead.

2. Play the song or the video clip. Then invite the participants to reflect on and journal about what it would have been like to experience this miracle that day. Ask them to remain quiet until this activity is over.

Break (2:30 P.M.)

Jesus Calms the Storm (3:00 P.M.)

Preparation

- Ask a team member to prepare a 15-minute talk on Jesus Calms the Storm. To help the person prepare, give him or her a copy of resource 11, "Suggestions for the Jesus Calms the Storm Talk," as well as a copy of appendix A, "Helpful Hints for Giving Talks."

1. Introduce the team member giving this talk.

2. After the talk, allow 5 minutes for quiet reflection and journal writing.

Islands of Safety (3:20 P.M.)

Preparation

- Gather the following supplies:
  - ❑ carpet squares, one for each retreatant (an alternative would be large pieces of construction paper)
  - ❑ a CD of sounds of the ocean or rainy or stormy weather
- Scatter the carpet squares around the room.

1. Invite everyone to stand on a piece of carpet, otherwise known as "their island of safety." Start playing the CD of ocean or storm sounds. Invite everyone to step off their island and walk around the room, weaving in and out of the carpet squares. While they are moving around the room, take away some of the carpet squares. Note that this activity is not intended to be a race to see who can get to a square first. Everyone must cooperate. It is important that there be no pushing or shoving. Stop the music and yell out: "Troubled waters! Everyone must find an island to stand on for safety! Some people will have to share islands!" Allow everyone to find an island on which to stand.

2. Start the music again and ask everyone to move around once more. Remove a few more carpet squares. Enlarge some of the islands by laying down extra carpet squares side by side. Stop the music and yell out: "Troubled waters! Again, everyone must find an island of safety to stand on!" Allow everyone to find an island to stand on.

3. Continue this for several rounds, until there is just one island left, a large island made up of one-third of the carpet squares.

4. Ask everyone to sit down. Pose the following questions to the large group:

- What did you learn from this activity?
- Who or what causes "troubled waters"?
- Who or what are our "islands of safety"?
- How can you make a connection between this game and the miracle of Jesus Calming the Storm?

(This activity is drawn from Lisa-Marie Calderone-Stewart, *Lights for the World: Training Youth Leaders for Peer Ministry*, pp. 62–63.)

Closing Liturgy (4:30 P.M.)

Celebrate the liturgy with the retreatants and, if you so choose, other parish members, such as family and friends of the retreatants. Before the recessional song, it would be appropriate to thank the team, give directions for dinner, and encourage the retreatants to continue living what they have learned and experienced during the retreat.

Dinner (5:30 P.M.)

Alternative Ideas for This Retreat

Here are some activities that can be used for a longer version of this retreat or as alternative activities:

- If someone in your parish has visited Lourdes or Fatima, invite them to share the history and tradition of the miracles first experienced there and their reflections on their visits to holy ground.
- If your parish or school has a patron saint, investigate the miracles connected with the saint's life. Ask someone to speak of how the Church investigates miracles during a person's path to sainthood.
- Allow the retreat team to choose different ways to present or proclaim each miracle in each section of the retreat, particularly if the team has a flair for drama.

Follow-Up Idea for This Retreat

Here is an idea for a follow-up activity for this retreat:

- Invite retreatants to choose a miracle that was not explored during the retreat and design their own activity, discussion, or game to bring the miracle to life.

Resource 3

Suggestions for Welcome and Opening Talk

This talk introduces the theme of the retreat, "It's a Miracle," to the retreatants and prepares them for what they are going to experience. You have about 20 minutes for this presentation. The following outline provides ideas and thought starters.

You Are a Miracle

- You are a unique creation of God. There is no one exactly like you.
- If you do not think you are a miracle, just take a moment to study the intricacies of your hands and fingers and think about all they can do. Listen to your breath go in and out for a few minutes.
- Every day that you wake up and get out of bed is a miracle.

Why Did Jesus Perform Miracles?

- Jesus performed miracles to help his followers believe but also to build faith. Even today, his miracles inspire and challenge us to believe.
- Jesus performed miracles to meet the very human needs of people—the need for food, the need for healing, and the need for safety.
- Miracles, like parables, were one of the ways Jesus taught people about the immeasurable love of God. They are a challenge to build the Reign of God.
- Even in Jesus's day, there were those who said, "I'll believe it when I see it." Jesus shares these miracles to help our unbelief. But we are called to move toward a deeper faith where we can believe without seeing.

Stories of Conversion

- Share a miracle from your own experience. It may be something as profound as surviving cancer, having a baby, finding true love, or being in a car accident and surviving serious injury.
- Every time we read about or hear proclaimed a miracle of Jesus, we should ask ourselves: What change takes place in this miracle? What needs to change in my life right now?

Miracles in Our Everyday Lives

- Jesus continues to perform miracles through other people. For example, Jesus heals us through doctors and those who find cures for disease. If you do not think of these actions as miracles, who do you think created doctors and scientists?
- How has your life been touched by Jesus? Count your blessings each day and see where Jesus is working.
- Share some miracles from your everyday life—the surprises, the blessings, the ways in which God touches you, and your experiences of wonder and awe.

Challenges for Our Retreat

- To believe in yourself—the difference you can make in the world around you.
- To believe in others—and allow them to touch your life.
- To believe in God—and open yourself up to the possibilities God has in store for you.

Closing Remarks

- If Jesus can turn water into wine and cause bread and fish to multiply, if Jesus can take human form and be born in a stable in Bethlehem, if Jesus can walk on water, imagine what Jesus can do with us.
- Be open to all we do in the next two days. Be open to learning more about yourself, others, and God.

Handout 8

Jesus and the Blind Man: Luke 18:35–43

Voice 1: A reading from the Gospel of Luke.

All: Praise to you, Lord, Jesus Christ.

Voice 2: As he approached Jericho, a blind man was sitting by the roadside begging. When he heard a crowd gong by, he asked what was happening. They told him,

Voices 3 and 4: "Jesus of Nazareth is passing by."

Voice 2: Then he shouted,

All: "Jesus, Son of David, have mercy on me!"

Voice 2: Those who were in front sternly ordered him to be quiet; but he shouted even more loudly,

All: "Son of David, have mercy on me!"

Voice 2: Jesus stood still and ordered that the man be brought to him; and when he came near, he asked him,

Voice 5: "What do you want me to do for you?"

Voice 2: He said,

All: "Lord, let me see again."

Voice 2: Jesus said to him,

Voice 5: "Receive your sight; your faith has saved you."

Voice 2: Immediately he regained his sight and followed him, glorifying God; and all the people, when they saw it, praised God.

Voice 1: The Gospel of the Lord.

All: Thanks be to God.

Resource 4

Take Off the Blindfolds

The blind man kept calling out to Jesus even when others told him to be quiet. What are some ways we can call out to God?

The man cured by Jesus suffered physical blindness. How are we sometimes blind to the Word of God?

What are some of the things that cause spiritual blindness?

How are we sometimes blind to the needs of the people around us?

How are we sometimes blind to the good in ourselves?

Jesus said, "What do you want me to do for you?" (Luke 18:41). How would you answer this question?

What do you think Jesus meant when he said, "Your faith has saved you" (Luke 18:42)?

If Jesus takes our blindfolds off, what will we see?

Resource 5

Suggestions for the Boy Cured of a Demon Talk

This talk explores the miracle of the Boy Cured of a Demon. You have about 15 minutes for the presentation. The following ideas and thought starters may be helpful.

Starting Point

- Proclaim Mark 9:14–29.

Message for Today

- In today's society, we face a lot of demons, both individually and as a society. The demons may be addictions or general ills of society. Give some examples of the demons facing individuals. Give some examples of the demons troubling our society.
- In this Scripture passage, Jesus speaks of a "faithless generation" (verse 19). How might this challenge be meant for us today?
- Jesus emphasizes the importance of having faith, yet we struggle with doubts from time to time. What can cause us to have doubts in ourselves? in others? in our God?
- What can we do to build our faith? to help it grow stronger? How can the support of our family faith community and parish faith community help us face our doubts?
- The father in this Scripture passage turned to Jesus when he needed help to heal his son. Jesus has the power to heal us. Let us turn to Jesus when we need help for ourselves or others.

Personal Connection

- Jesus has the power to heal us, to help us overcome our bad habits and our troubles. How can we call on Jesus to help us meet our goals to be better people, to eat healthier food, to say no to drugs, to exercise more, to put out our cigarettes? In your own life, how have you asked for God's help?
- We can help others struggling through tough times. We must do what we can but also recognize our limits. Why is it important to get help for someone suffering from a serious demon such as depression, anorexia, or alcoholism, rather than just trying to help him or her ourselves? Share a time when you helped someone through a crisis.
- Jesus says, "All things can be done for the one who believes" (Mark 9:23). Share a time when your faith has helped you get through a tough time in your life.

Handout 9

Pray It! Study It! Live It!

The Miracle of the Boy Cured of a Demon
Mark 9:14–29

Study It! What can we learn from this miracle Scripture?

Live It! How does this miracle Scripture call us to live?

Pray It! What can we bring from this Scripture to prayer?

Resource 6

Prayer to Cast Out Demons: Mark 9:14–29

Reader 1: When they came to the disciples, they saw a great crowd around them, and some scribes arguing with them. When the whole crowd saw him, they were immediately overcome with awe, and they ran forward to greet him.

Reader 2: He asked them, "What are you arguing about with them?"

Reader 3: Someone from the crowd answered him, "Teacher, I brought you my son; he has a spirit that makes him unable to speak; and whenever it seizes him, it dashes him down; and he foams and grinds his teeth and becomes rigid; and I asked your disciples to cast it out, but they could not do so."

Reader 2: He answered them, "You faithless generation. How much longer must I be among you? How much longer must I put up with you? Bring him to me."

Reader 1: And they brought the boy to him. When the spirit saw him, immediately it convulsed the boy, and he fell on the ground and rolled about, foaming at the mouth.

Reader 2: Jesus asked the father, "How long has this been happening to him?"

Reader 3: And he said, "From childhood. It has often cast him into the fire and into the water, to destroy him; but if you are able to do anything, have pity on us and help us."

Reader 2: "If you are able! All things can be done for the one who believes."

Reader 3: Immediately the father of the child cried out, "I believe; help my unbelief!"

Reader 1: Then Jesus rebuked the unclean spirit, saying to it:

Reader 2: "You spirit who keeps this boy from speaking and hearing, I command you, come out of him, and never enter him again!"

Reader 1: After crying out and convulsing him terribly, it came out, and the boy was like a corpse, so that most of them said, "He is dead." But Jesus took him by the hand and lifted him up, and he was able to stand.

Reader 4: When he had entered the house, his disciples asked him privately, "Why could we not cast it out?"

Reader 2: He said to them, "This kind can come out only through prayer."

Resource 7

Fishbowl Questions

Name a song title or book title that has the word *miracle* in it.

What is your favorite miracle story? Why?

Why do you think Jesus performed miracles?

I think it is a miracle that . . .

I am awed by the miracle of God's creation when . . .

What is one way you can be a "miracle worker" with Jesus?

Why is our world today so much in need of miracles?

One thing I learned yesterday was . . .

Today, I pray that . . .

I can share Jesus's gift of healing by . . .

Name three miracles that Jesus performed.

(This resource is adapted from Maryann Hakowski, *Growing with Jesus: Sixteen Half-Day, Full-Day, and Overnite Retreats That Help Children Celebrate and Share the Light of Christ* [Notre Dame, IN: Ave Maria Press, 1993], pages 147–148. Copyright © 1993 by Ave Maria Press.)

Resource 8

Suggestions for the Loaves and Fish Talk

This talk explores the miracle of the Loaves and Fish. You have about 15 minutes for the presentation. The following ideas and thought starters may be helpful.

Starting Point

- Proclaim Matthew 14:13–21.
  (This miracle can also be found in Mark 6:30–44, Luke 9:10–17, and John 6:1–15.)

Message for Today

- Many of the miracles help us connect with Jesus's great love for us. Jesus does not want us to go hungry. We are fed through the gift of the Gospel message of Christ, the gift of God's word. We are nourished by the Body of Christ in the Eucharist.
- Jesus feeds us, physically and spiritually, every time we receive the Eucharist. In this miracle Scripture, the five loaves and two fish change into enough food to feed thousands. In the Eucharist, we experience an incredible miracle. The bread and wine become the Body and Blood of Christ.
- Sometimes we think we have nothing to offer. Our pockets are empty and we feel empty. But Jesus says that even six loaves and two fish will do.

Personal Connection

- Share a time when you helped prepare a meal at the soup kitchen or packed Christmas food baskets for needy families or made sandwiches for homeless people.
- Share a time when you were able to give someone a spiritual boost. How were you able to give someone's spirit a lift with help from the Holy Spirit?

Handout 10

Blessing Bread, Breaking Bread, Sharing Bread

Blessing Bread

Please plan the first part of the morning prayer. Your theme is "Blessing the Bread." Everyone in your group must contribute to the planning of the prayer and help in some way in sharing it with others. Here are a few ideas to get you started thinking about the theme:

- Consider a Scripture passage (or two) that focuses on blessing bread. (Check with the other two groups to be sure you are not selecting the same passage.)
- Consider a gathering song that would be appropriate for the theme.
- Consider an opening prayer or greeting that would be appropriate for the theme.
- What symbols might you use to help set the environment?

Breaking Bread

Please plan the second part of the morning prayer. Your theme is "Breaking the Bread." Everyone in your group must contribute to the planning of the prayer and help in some way in sharing it with others. Here are some ideas to get you started thinking about the theme:

- Consider a Scripture passage that focuses on blessing bread. (Check with the other two groups to be sure you are not selecting the same passage.)
- Consider a song or psalm response that would be appropriate for this portion of the prayer.
- Consider sharing a story about a special family meal where you broke bread together. Or consider sharing a reflection focusing on these questions:
  - How are we all "broken" in some ways?
  - Who are the "broken people" for whom you would like to pray?

Sharing Bread

Please plan the last part of the morning prayer. Your theme is "Sharing Bread." Everyone in your group must contribute to the planning of the prayer and help in some way in sharing it with others. Here are some ideas to get you started thinking about the theme:

- Consider a Scripture passage that focuses on blessing bread. (Check with the other two groups to be sure you are not selecting the same passage.)
- Consider including some type of ritual action (such as breaking and sharing bread). If you choose to break and share bread, be sure you explain that this is not the same as the Eucharist but rather a symbolic gesture.
- Consider including a prayer that challenges all of us to share what we have with those in need.
- Consider a song that would be appropriate for the conclusion of the prayer.

Resource 9

The Wedding Feast at Cana: John 2:1–11

Voice 1: A reading from the Gospel of John.

All: Praise to you, Lord, Jesus Christ.

Voice 2: On the third day there was a wedding in Cana of Galilee, and the mother of Jesus was there. Jesus and his disciples had also been invited to the wedding. When the wine gave out, the mother of Jesus said to him,

Voice 3: "They have no wine."

Voice 2: And Jesus said to her,

Voice 4: "Woman, what concern is that to you and to me? My hour has not yet come."

Voice 2: His mother said to the servants,

Voice 3: "Do whatever he tells you."

Voice 2: Now standing there were six stone water jars for the Jewish rites of purification, each holding twenty or thirty gallons. Jesus said to them,

Voice 4: "Fill the jars with water."

Voice 2: And they filled them up to the brim. He said to them,

Voice 4: "Now draw some out, and take it to the chief steward."

Voice 2: So they took it. When the steward tasted the water that had become wine, and did not know where it came from, the steward called to the bridegroom and said to him,

All: "Everyone serves the good wine first, and the inferior wine after the guests have become drunk. But you have kept the good wine until now."

Voice 2: Jesus did this, the first of his signs, in Cana of Galilee, and revealed his glory; and his disciples believed in him.

Voice 1: The Gospel of the Lord.

All: Praise to you, Lord, Jesus Christ.

Resource 10

Questions in Clay Pots

Why do you think Jesus changed the water into wine?

Why do you think Jesus was reluctant to say yes to his mother's request?

What miracle takes place in this Scripture reading?

Give another example of a miracle performed by Jesus.

Why do you think Jesus performed miracles?

How does Jesus transform wine every time we celebrate the Eucharist?

How can you relate this miracle to your everyday life?

How would you have reacted if you had been a guest at this wedding feast?

Jesus came to the rescue of the couple when they ran out of wine. How might you rescue someone in need?

Handout 11

Jesus Raises Lazarus from the Dead: John 11:1–44

Voice 1: A reading from the Gospel of John.

All: Praise to you, Lord, Jesus Christ.

Voice 2: Now a certain man was ill, Lazarus of Bethany, the village of Mary, and her sister Martha. Mary was the one who anointed the Lord with perfume and wiped his feet with her hair; her brother Lazarus was ill. So the sisters sent a message to Jesus,

All: "Lord, he whom you love is ill."

Voice 2: But when Jesus heard it, he said,

Voice 3: "This illness does not lead to death; rather it is for God's glory, so that the Son of God may be glorified through it."

Voice 2: Accordingly, though Jesus loved Martha and her sister and Lazarus, after having heard that Lazarus was ill, he stayed two days longer in the place where he was. Then, after this, he said to the disciples,

Voice 3: "Let us go to Judea again."

Voice 2: The disciples said to him,

Voices 4 and 5: "Rabbi, the Jews were just now trying to stone you, and are you going there again?"

Voice 2: Jesus answered,

Voice 3: "Are there not twelve hours of daylight? Those who walk during the day do not stumble, because they see the light of the world. But those who walk at night stumble, because the light is not in them."

Voice 2: After saying this, he told them,

Voice 3: "Our friend Lazarus has fallen asleep, but I am going there to awaken him."

Voice 2: The disciples said to him,

Voices 4 and 5: "Lord, if he has fallen asleep, he will be all right."

Voice 2: Jesus, however, had been speaking about his death, but they thought he was referring merely to sleep. Then Jesus told them plainly,

Voice 3: "Lazarus is dead. For your sake I am glad I was not there, so that you may believe. But let us go to him."

Voice 2: Thomas, who was called the Twin, said to his fellow disciples,

Voice 4: "Let us also go, and die with him."

Voice 2: When Jesus arrived, he found that Lazarus had already been in the tomb for four days. Now, Bethany was near Jerusalem, some two miles away. And many of the Jews had come to Mary and Martha to console them about their brother. When Martha heard that Jesus was coming, she went and met him, while Mary stayed at home. Martha said to Jesus,

All: "Lord, if you had been here, my brother would not have died. But even now I know that God will give you whatever you ask of him."

Voice 2: Jesus said to her,

Voice 3: "Your brother will rise again."

Voice 2: Martha said to him,

All: "I know that he will rise again in the resurrection on the last day."

Voice 2: Jesus said to her,

Voice 3: "I am the resurrection and the life. Those who believe in me, even though they die, will live, and everyone who lives and believes in me will never die. Do you believe this?"

Voice 2: She said to him,

All: "Yes, Lord, I believe that you are the Messiah, the Son of God, the one coming into the world."

Voice 2: When she had said this, she went back and called her sister Mary, and told her privately,

All: "The Teacher is here and is calling for you."

Voice 2: And when she heard it, she got up quickly and went to him. Now Jesus had not yet come into the village, but was still at the place where Martha had met him. The Jews who were with her in the house, consoling her, saw Mary get up quickly and go out. They followed her because they thought she was going to the tomb to weep there. When Mary came to where Jesus was and saw him, she knelt at his feet and said to him,

All: "Lord, if you had been here, my brother would not have died."

Voice 2: When Jesus saw her weeping, and the Jews who came with her also weeping, he was greatly disturbed in spirit and deeply moved. He said,

Voice 3: "Where have you laid him?"

Voice 2: They said to him,

All: "Lord, come and see."

Voice 2: Jesus began to weep. So the Jews said,

Voices 6 and 7: "See how he loved him!"

Voices 2: But some of them said,

Voices 6 and 7: "Could not he who opened the eyes of the blind man have kept this man from dying?"

Voice 2: Then Jesus, again greatly disturbed, came to the tomb. It was a cave, and a stone was lying against it. Jesus said,

Voice 3 "Take away the stone."

Voice 2: Martha, the sister of the dead man, said to him,

All: "Lord, already there is a stench because he has been dead for four days."

Voice 2: Jesus said to her,

Voice 3: "Did I not tell you that if you believed, you would see the glory of God?"

Voice 2: So they took away the stone. And Jesus looked upward and said,

Voice 3: "Father, I thank you for having heard me. I knew that you always hear me, but I have said this for the sake of the crowd standing here, so that they may believe that you have sent me."

Voice 2: When he had said this, he cried with a loud voice,

Voice 3: "Lazarus, come out!"

Voice 2: The dead man came out, his hands and feet bound with strips of cloth, and his face wrapped in a cloth. Jesus said to them,

Voice 3: "Unbind him, and let him go."

Voice 1: The Word of the Lord.

All: Thanks be to God.

Resource 11

Suggestions for the Jesus Calms the Storm Talk

This talk explores the miracle of Jesus Calming the Storm. You have about 15 minutes for the presentation. The following ideas and thought starters may be helpful.

Starting Point

- Proclaim Mark 4:35–41.
  (This miracle can be also found in Matthew 8:23–27 and Luke 8:22–25.)

Message for Today

- How can living out our faith in Jesus bring a calming sense of peace into our lives? How can we be a sign of peace to our families and friends?
- We all face storms. Some may be short. Others go on for days or months. Some of us deal with stormy relationships. Talk about some of the things you can do to calm stormy relationships. You might begin by talking about compromise, communication, and compassion.
- Jesus is the calm before the storm, the calm during the storm, and the calm after the storm. Do not be afraid to get into the boat with Jesus. He will always be there for you.
- Why do we sometimes feel that Jesus is asleep in the boat as waves are crashing around us? Jesus tells us not to be afraid. He will be with us. We need to be steadfast in our faith and have confidence that our God will save us.

Personal Connection

- Share a time when you encountered a frightening storm in your life. How did your faith help keep you safe from the storm? How were your friends and family islands of safety for you to cling to during the storm?
- What can we do to praise and worship a God so great "that even the wind and the sea obey him" (Mark 4:41)?
- Why are we sometimes afraid to rock the boat? Give an example of a time when it was tough to stand up for what you believe.

Retreat 4

It's Cool to Be Catholic

Introduction

"It's Cool to Be Catholic" is an overnight retreat that invites young people to celebrate their Catholic faith and build identity and pride in being Catholic. It welcomes those first learning about the faith as well as those seeking to move to a deeper level of faith.

Goals

- To build excitement about Catholic faith.
- To build appreciation of traditional Catholic prayers and devotions.
- To offer an opportunity for individual and communal prayer and to expand the personal prayer life of retreatants.
- To celebrate the joys and understand some of the challenges of living as a Catholic Christian.
- To gain a deeper insight into the liturgical year and how the seasons of the Church are part of the fabric of our faith life.

Schedule

The following sequence for "It's Cool to Be Catholic" is just one suggestion on how to arrange your schedule. Use the column labeled "Actual Plan" to record the activities, sequences, and starting times that will work for you.

Time	*Activity Name*	*Activity Type*	*Actual Plan*
Friday evening			
6:30 P.M.	Arrival		______
6:50 P.M.	Welcome and Opening Talk	Theme talk	______
7:10 P.M.	Liturgical Colors	Small-group formation	______
7:20 P.M.	Bingo	Icebreaker	______
7:45 P.M.	There Is Nothing Ordinary About Ordinary Time	Prayer point	______
7:55 P.M.	This Is What We Believe	Activity and discussion	______
8:25 P.M.	Of Water and Light	Prayer	______
8:45 P.M.	Snack Break		______
9:15 P.M.	It's Advent: Do You Know Who You Are Waiting For?	Prayer point	______
9:25 P.M.	Inside and Outside the Box	Activity	______
9:55 P.M.	What Do You Really Want for Christmas?	Quiet reflection	______
10:30 P.M.	Break		______
10:40 P.M.	Why I Am a Catholic: Talk 1	Witness talk	______
11:00 P.M.	A Living Rosary	Night prayer	______
12:00 A.M.	Lights Out		______
Saturday			
7:45 A.M.	Rising		______
8:30 A.M.	Breakfast		______
9:00 A.M.	Name That Catholic Tune	Icebreaker	______
9:30 A.M.	The Journey Through Lent to the Cross	Prayer point	______
9:40 A.M.	Heart to Heart: A Call to Outreach	Activity	______
10:25 A.M.	Break		______
10:55 A.M.	Catholic Social Teaching: A Call to Justice	Activity and discussion	______
11:40 A.M.	Why I Am a Catholic: Talk 2	Witness talk	______
12:00 P.M.	Saints and Sinners	Prayer	______

12:30 P.M.	Lunch		______
1:15 P.M.	Name That Sacrament	Icebreaker	______
1:45 P.M.	We Are an Easter People; We Are a Sacramental People	Prayer point	______
1:55 P.M.	Why I Am a Catholic: Talk 3	Witness talk	______
2:15 P.M.	Signs and Wonders	Prayer	______
3:00 P.M.	Free Time		______
4:15 P.M.	The Spirit Moves Us: The Call of Pentecost	Prayer point	______
4:30 P.M.	Witness Wear	Activity	______
5:30 P.M.	Dinner		______
6:15 P.M.	Preparation for Liturgy		______
7:00 P.M.	Closing Liturgy		______

General Materials and Preparation

- The suggested space needs for this retreat include a large gathering space, tables for small groups, and a designated prayer space.
- Gather the following items:
  - ❑ clear pin-back name tags, one for each person
  - ❑ paper in the following colors: green, purple, light purple, pink, red, white, cream
- Before the retreat, assign retreatants to small groups of approximately eight people. Assign one teen team member and one adult team member to each group.
- Assign each group one of the colors and seasons:
  - ❑ Ordinary Time: green
  - ❑ Advent: purple
  - ❑ Advent: pink
  - ❑ Christmas: white
  - ❑ Lent: purple
  - ❑ Easter: white
  - ❑ Easter: red
- Create a name tag for each person at the retreat, matching the color background of the name tag to the color of each person's group.
- Ask each person to bring a shoe box to the retreat. Ask team members to bring extra shoe boxes in case any of the retreatants forget them.
- Create a portable supply basket for each small group, containing the following frequently used items:
  - ❑ pens or pencils
  - ❑ markers
  - ❑ scissors

- ❏ glue sticks
- ❏ self-stick notes
- ❏ participant journals or blank sheets of paper
- ❏ songbooks or hymnals
- ❏ copies of *The Catholic Youth Bible* or another Bible

- Place a basket at each group table.

Detailed Description of Activities for Friday

Welcome and Opening Talk (6:50 p.m.)

Preparation

- Ask a team member to prepare a 20-minute opening talk to introduce the theme of the retreat. To help the person prepare, give her or him a copy of resource 12, "Suggestions for the Welcome and Opening Talk," as well as a copy of appendix A, "Helpful Hints for Giving Talks."

1. After all the retreatants arrive, welcome everyone and introduce the retreat team. Distribute name tags if you have not already done so. Then introduce the person giving the welcome talk. After she or he is finished, review the retreat ground rules and make any needed announcements.

Liturgical Colors (7:10 p.m.)

1. Direct retreatants to look at the colors of the name tags they received when they arrived. Direct them to find people who have name tags of the same color and then find a table and sit down together. Invite them to introduce themselves to the members of their new group. Tell them this will be their small group for all retreat activities and discussions.

2. Now, offer some comments about liturgical seasons:

   When you think of a year, probably the calendar year or maybe the academic year pops into your head. But the Church has a special year, called the liturgical year, to mark the celebration of its liturgies. The liturgical year celebrates God's time, which is eternal and infinite. We do this by remembering the past, celebrating the present, and looking toward the future.

   The liturgical year is built around important historical events, such as the birth, death, and Resurrection of Jesus, in which God's saving power was made real. The liturgies in the liturgical year help us remember God's saving power made real in those historical events. (*CFH*, pp.138–139)

   Throughout the year, we see the colors of the seasons change as the priest puts on different vestments and the worship space at church is adorned with different cloths.

Bingo (7:20 P.M.)

Preparation

- Gather the following supplies:
  - ❏ a small portable Bingo game borrowed from the church or school or an inexpensive Bingo game purchased from a toy or game store
  - ❏ copies of handout 12, "Cool Bingo Questions," one for each retreatant
- Place Bingo tokens or markers on the tables.
- Designate a team member to serve as the Bingo caller.

1. Distribute a copy of handout 12 to each retreatant. Introduce this activity in the following way:

   We will play Bingo together tonight. Our greatest prize, by far, will be the chance to get to know one another better. If you have one of the numbers called, introduce yourself to the other members of your small group and then answer one of the questions on your handout. You can choose any question you like. Be sure to claim the number called by placing a marker or token on your actual card.

2. Invite the team member who is the Bingo caller to begin calling out numbers. Be sure to allow time between calls for table sharing. Ask table leaders to raise their hands when their group has finished discussing a question and is ready for the next number.

3. When someone yells "Bingo," invite that person to stand up, introduce himself or herself to the entire group, and answer one of the questions on the handout.

4. Close by thanking retreatants for sharing their answers.

There Is Nothing Ordinary About Ordinary Time (7:45 P.M.)

Preparation

- Gather the following supplies:
  - ❏ a tabletop water fountain or a clear glass bowl full of water
  - ❏ a crucifix
- Place the fountain or bowl of water on a table in a location where all can see it.

1. Introduce this prayer point in the following way:
   (Put your hand in the bowl of water, and let the water flow through your fingers.)

   Sometimes we take water for granted. It is an ordinary part of our lives. We drink it, cook with it, wash in it, and swim in it, but we rarely think much about it. It is always there. Jesus took the ordinary elements of life, such as water, and used them to teach people about the Reign of God. He changed water into wine, walked on water, and calmed the water of a raging sea.

2. Proclaim Matthew 3:13–17. Allow a few moments of silence following the proclamation.

3. Place a crucifix on the table by the bowl of water where all can see it. Then continue with these comments:

   We generally have a routine that helps us do the ordinary things that make up daily life. This routine is needed so that we can integrate some of the lessons and experiences we have experienced during times of joy and new life, or sadness and loss. The liturgical year has the same balance. After the high of the Christmas season, we enter a short period of Ordinary Time.

   During Ordinary Time, the Scripture readings focus on the events of the life of Jesus between his birth and his death and Resurrection. It is a time when we reflect on the way Jesus lived and the things he taught, so that we might make our values and attitudes more like his. Ordinary Time is divided into two periods. The first period is between Christmastime and Lent, and the second period is between the end of the Easter season and Advent. (*CFH*, pp. 140–141)

   During this retreat, we will immerse ourselves in the stories of Jesus—the stories he lived and the stories he told. As we connect them to our everyday lives, we too can see beyond the ordinary in our lives and become extraordinary, transformed by walking with Jesus.

   And so we pray in the name of the Father, and of the Son, and of the Holy Spirit.

   God, we call on you to bless us with open minds and hearts, that we may find you everywhere and in everything and everyone. We ask this through Christ, our Lord. Amen.

This Is What We Believe (7:55 P.M.)

Preparation

- Gather the following supplies:
  - ❑ Play-Doh, two or three cans for each small group
  - ❑ pipe cleaners, several for each small group
  - ❑ poster board, one sheet for each small group
  - ❑ Legos, enough for each group to have an ample set
  - ❑ crayons, one box for each small group
  - ❑ copies of handout 13, "The Creed," one for each person
- Place the assortment of creative and craft materials and building supplies on a supply table at the front of the room.

1. Distribute copies of handout 13 to each retreatant. Introduce the activity in the following way:

   Who are we as Catholics? What do we believe? A good place to start is with our statement of belief, the creed we pray every Sunday with our Catholic community at Mass.

   When we pray the creed, we proclaim together our belief in the Trinity—the Father, Son, and Holy Spirit—and the importance of the

Catholic Church in God's plan. We stand as a community when we pray the creed, so we are, in a way, "standing up for what we believe."

Some of us have prayed the creed many times, perhaps hundreds of times. Because we are quick to recite it, we often take the words and their meaning for granted. Let us pray the prayer together now, a little slower than usual, and really think about the words as we pray them.

2. After finishing the prayer, invite the groups to choose two or three lines of the creed for further reflection. Allow a few moments for the groups to decide. Tell the groups they will have 20 minutes to do the following:
   - Reflect on what that part of the creed means.
   - Find a creative way to share this meaning with the large group.

   They can use Legos or pipe cleaners, crayons or markers, Play-Doh or any of the other creative materials available at the supply table. They can make up a crossword puzzle, write a skit, create a symbol, or write a song. Urge them to use their imagination.

3. When 20 minutes have passed, gather the groups together so they can share their creations and insights with the large group.

4. Close by encouraging all to make the creed more than just words they recite once a week.

Of Water and Light (8:25 P.M.)

Preparation

- Gather the following supplies:
  - ❑ an Easter candle or a large white pillar candle
  - ❑ taper candles, one for each person
  - ❑ a CD recording of "Creed" (from the collection titled *Offerings II: All I Have to Give*, by Third Day [Brentwood Publishing, 2003]) or another contemporary Christian song that reflects the importance of expressing what we believe as Catholic Christians
  - ❑ a CD player
  - ❑ a bowl of holy water
  - ❑ a basket (large enough to hold all the taper candles)
  - ❑ three copies of resource 13, "Of Water and Light"
- Put the taper candles in the basket.
- Recruit three team members to serve as prayer leaders. Give each a copy of resource 13 and assign each person a part.

1. Invite the retreatants to join you in the prayer space. Allow a few moments for everyone to get settled. Then proceed with the prayer as outlined on resource 13.

Snack Break (8:45 P.M.)

It's Advent: Do You Know Who You Are Waiting For? (9:15 P.M.)

Preparation

- Gather the following supplies:
  - ❏ a party noisemaker
  - ❏ an Advent wreath, four candles (three purple, one pink), and matches
  - ❏ songbooks with the song "O Come, O Come, Emmanuel," one for each retreatant

1. Introduce this prayer point in the following way:
(*Blow a noisemaker very loudly to get the attention of the retreatants.*)

   Happy New Year! The liturgical year begins in late November or early December, on the fourth Sunday before Christmas. The four weeks before Christmas make up the liturgical season of Advent. *Advent* means "coming," and this season is a preparation for the coming of the infant Jesus. The mood is hopeful anticipation, and the Scripture readings focus on God's promise to send a savior to deliver us from sin and death. It is a time to take life a little more slowly and to focus on what we need to do to allow God to more fully enter our hearts. This is a challenge in our culture, with all the shopping trips that people make and all the concerts and parties that people attend during this time. (*CFH*, pp. 139–140)

   When we celebrate the new calendar year on January 1, we often make resolutions, letting go of the old and welcoming the new. The season of Advent is a time of preparation for the birth of Jesus Christ. Advent is a time to change our hearts, to think about how we can become better people.

2. Proclaim Matthew 3:1–11. Allow a few moments of silence following the proclamation.

3. Light the Advent wreath, and continue with these comments:

   The colors of the liturgical season of Advent are purple and pink. The candles of the Advent wreath represent peace, hope, joy, and love. The purple candles are lit on the first, second, and fourth Sundays and the pink one on the third Sunday. We light one candle on the first Sunday of Advent and add a candle each week.

4. Close by inviting the participants to open their songbooks and join in singing "O Come, O Come, Emmanuel."

Inside and Outside the Box (9:25 P.M.)

Preparation

- Gather the following supplies:
  - ❑ shoe boxes, one for each retreatant
  - ❑ fine-tip markers
  - ❑ solid-colored wrapping paper, enough for each person to wrap the outside of his or her shoe box
  - ❑ tape, one roll for each small group
  - ❑ scissors, one pair for each small group
  - ❑ slips of paper
- Ask a team member to complete this activity before the retreat and have her or his shoe box ready to show the group as an example.

1. Introduce this activity in the following way:

   > Advent is a time of waiting, a time of anticipation. But what are we to do while we are waiting? The prophet Isaiah tells us that John the Baptist was sent to be "the voice of one crying out in the wilderness: 'Prepare the way of the Lord, make his paths straight'" (Matthew 3:3). We are called to change our lives. And we do not have to wait for Advent to look at ourselves and change for the better.
   >
   > What does it mean to think outside the box? It means to find a new way of thinking, to find a new way of doing things. Most people spend the weeks before Christmas in a mad scramble of consumerism. As Catholic Christians, we are invited to think outside the gift box and prepare ourselves for the coming of Christ.

2. Provide each retreatant with a shoe box and a sheet of wrapping paper. Provide each small group with some markers, a roll of tape, and a pair of scissors. Invite the retreatants to wrap their boxes with the wrapping paper. Note that they should cut a hole in the top of the box large enough so they can drop small slips of paper inside. Allow about 5 minutes for them to complete this portion of the activity.

3. Ask the retreatants to write on the outside of the box ways they can change themselves on the outside. Explain that you are not speaking about their outward appearance but about ways in which they interact with other people. Give some examples, such as, "I will try to treat my parents with more respect," "I will try to get my homework done on time", "I will offer to help others before they ask me." Allow some time for them to complete this task.

4. Now ask the retreatants to write on slips of paper ways they can change on the inside. Give some examples: "I will stop being so tough on myself and build my self-esteem," "I will try to pray a little each day", "I will stop listening to music with negative messages." Tell them to drop these ideas into their boxes. Again, allow some time for them to complete this task.

5. If time permits, invite the small groups to do some sharing among themselves. Then close by telling the retreatants that they do not have to wait until Advent to make a change in their lives. Encourage them to follow through on some of the goals written on their box and on the slips of paper in their box.

What Do You Really Want for Christmas? (9:55 P.M.)

Preparation

- Gather the following supplies:
  - ❑ large mailing envelopes, one for each retreatant
  - ❑ a CD player (optional)
  - ❑ a CD of reflective instrumental music (optional)

1. Introduce this activity in the following way:

   Christmas seems to come earlier and earlier each year. Then the push is to shop, shop, shop and buy, buy, buy to get more stuff, stuff, stuff. The Church's celebration of Advent stands in stark contrast to the secular holiday. After December 25, secular society takes down the Christmas lights and the holiday is over. The Church's season of Christmas starts on December 25 and ends two weeks later, on Epiphany.

   How many of you make a list each year of what you want for Christmas? Okay. Well, we are going to challenge you to write a very different Christmas wish list by asking yourself these questions:

   - What gifts of myself can I give for Christmas?
   - How can I give of myself to serve God and others?

2. Ask the retreatants to take a couple of blank sheets of paper and a pen and find a quiet place in the room where they can have some space to themselves. Provide each person with a blank envelope.

3. Invite them to create two different lists based on the questions you posed in step 1. You may wish to note the questions on newsprint. When they are finished, they should write their complete name and mailing address on the envelope and seal their lists inside. Note the importance of remaining quiet during the entire activity, even if some people finish before others. You may wish to play a CD of reflective instrumental music during this time.

Break (10:30 P.M.)

Why I Am a Catholic: Talk 1 (10:40 P.M.)

Preparation

- Ask someone who has been a Catholic since infancy to prepare a 15-minute talk on why he or she is Catholic. To help the person prepare, give him or her a copy of resource 14, "Suggestions for the Why I Am a Catholic Talk (Talks 1, 2, and 3)," as well as a copy of appendix A, "Helpful Hints for Giving Talks."

1. Introduce the team member giving this talk.

2. After the talk, allow 5 minutes for quiet reflection and journal writing.

A Living Rosary (11:00 P.M.)

Preparation

- Gather the following supplies:
  - ❑ rosaries, one for each retreatant
  - ❑ six large red candles
  - ❑ twenty-eight small blue votive candles
  - ❑ a processional cross or crucifix
  - ❑ thirty-five copies of resource 15, "A Living Rosary"
- For this prayer service, several young people will need to participate as prayer leaders. You will need six young people to lead the Lord's Prayer; give each of these people a red candle. You will need twenty-eight young people to lead one Hail Mary; give each one a blue candle. If the group is small, you can double up on assignments. You will also need one person to hold the processional cross or crucifix. Take time to practice both prayers with each prayer leader before beginning the service. Provide each with a copy of resource 15.

1. Invite the retreatants to join you in the prayer space. Provide each with a rosary. Allow a few moments for everyone to get settled. Then introduce this prayer in the following way:

   We gather to pray the rosary, a powerful devotion to Mary, the Blessed Mother, a favorite prayer of the Pope and a beloved Catholic tradition. The Church honors Mary as the mother of Jesus but also as the mother of our Church. This distinguishes us from other Christians. However, we do not adore Mary. We ask her to intercede for us with her son, Jesus Christ.

   The recitation of the rosary begins with a series of prayers said in order. A small chain of beads with a crucifix is used as a guide.

   After these introductory prayers have been said, the recitation of the decades begins. Five sets of ten Hail Marys are said. Each decade begins with an Our Father and concludes with a Glory Be. We keep track of the prayers said by moving from one bead to the next in order.

   The rosary is intended to move us to meditate on the mysteries of Jesus's life. The saying of a five-decade rosary is connected with meditation on what are called the mysteries of the life of Jesus. These mysteries are also collected in series of fives: five joyful, five sorrowful, and five glorious mysteries.

Praying the Hail Mary repeatedly helps a person to quietly reflect on these mysteries in order to enter into the life of Jesus. (*CFH*, pp. 307 and 385)

As we move from Advent to Christmas during our retreat, we will pray the joyous mysteries, which begin with the Annunciation and include the birth of Jesus.

2. Ask the retreatants to stand and form a "living rosary." The prayer leaders (i.e., the six people with red candles and the twenty-eight with blue candles) should place themselves among the other participants to help form the living rosary. Each person represents one of the beads of the rosary. Continue with the prayer as noted on resource 15.

Lights Out (12:00 A.M.)

Detailed Description of Activities for Saturday

Rising (7:45 A.M.)

Breakfast (8:30 A.M.)

Name That Catholic Tune (9:00 A.M.)

Preparation

- Ask the music or choir director for a list of the songs most commonly sung at Sunday liturgies. You will need to be familiar with each of these tunes (or find a team member who is) so that you can sing some of the lines of each song.

1. Invite the retreatants to gather in their small groups. Greet everyone by singing the first line of an upbeat, lively hymn or song. Ask the retreatants to finish the song and then "name that Catholic tune." Choose a second one, and ask them to respond again.

2. After you have given them two examples, ask the groups to make a list of at least three of their favorite songs or hymns. Note that they will need to be able to sing at least a few lines of the songs they choose. Allow about 10 minutes for them to compile their lists.

3. Invite each group to challenge the others: One group sings part of a song they have chosen. The others try to respond by singing more of the song or giving the title of the song. (Or the challenging group gives the title of the song.) The group then sings their second song, and their third song. When one group has sung all three of its songs and the others have responded, another group sings its songs, until all the groups have had a chance to sing their songs.

4. Thank everyone for participating. Close by encouraging the retreatants to join in the singing whenever they gather with the community for Mass. It is an important part of our Eucharistic celebration. Ask them to give their best efforts to all of the retreat activities for the day.

The Journey Through Lent to the Cross (9:30 A.M.)

Preparation

- Gather the following supplies:
  - ❑ a pair of old, well-worn tan or brown sandals
  - ❑ a wooden cross (not a crucifix)
  - ❑ copies of handout 14, "The Second Station of the Cross: Jesus Is Made to Take Up His Cross," one for each retreatant

1. Introduce this prayer point in the following way:

   Lent is a solemn, reflective season of the liturgical year during which we prepare for the mysteries of Easter. It begins on Ash Wednesday and lasts for forty days, until Easter (the forty days do not include the Sundays during Lent). On Ash Wednesday, people come to Church to receive ashes on the forehead, a reminder that without God we are simply dust. The forty days of Lent recall the forty days Jesus spent in the desert before beginning his public ministry. During Lent, Christians are called to renew themselves through fasting, prayer, and almsgiving, that is, giving money and service to those in need.

   The Lenten journey, from Ash Wednesday through Holy Week, is an invitation to walk in the shoes of Jesus. To walk with Jesus. To carry his cross. To allow him to carry our crosses. It is a special time for Catholics, marked by prayer, fasting, and almsgiving.

   These simple sandals remind us to seek a simpler life, a life in which God returns to the center, where God belongs. And fasting can be far more than giving up your favorite soda for Lent. We can fast from TV, video games, the Internet, the iPod, or whatever distracts us from God. If we walk with Jesus, we will not be able to walk by a person in need. Almsgiving is so much more than putting money in the poor box. We have to walk the walk with Jesus, not just talk the talk.

2. Proclaim John 19:1–6,14–19. Allow a few moments of silence following the proclamation.

3. Hold up the large wooden cross. Ask everyone to come forward and stand around it. Provide each person with a copy of handout 14 and invite them to join in the prayer as noted on the handout.

Heart to Heart: A Call to Outreach (9:40 A.M.)

Preparation

- Gather the following supplies:
  - ❏ newsprint
  - ❏ copies of handout 15, "The Two Feet of Christian Service," one for each retreatant
- Write each of the works of mercy on a separate sheet of newsprint:
  - ❏ feed the hungry
  - ❏ give drink to the thirsty
  - ❏ shelter the homeless
  - ❏ clothe the naked
  - ❏ care for the sick
  - ❏ help the imprisoned
  - ❏ bury the dead
- Post the sheets of newsprint in visible locations throughout the room.

1. Choose one of the following options to help retreatants identify ways to put the works of mercy into action. Choose the one that best fits the experience of the retreatants and the outreach charism of your parish or school.
   - Ask the retreatants to move freely around the room and write examples of how the parish reaches out under the appropriate work of mercy. For example, they can write "helping out at the soup kitchen" under "feed the hungry." Or "serving as an altar server for a funeral liturgy" under "bury the dead."
   - Give an overview of Catholic Relief Services and their work worldwide. You can start with Operation Rice Bowl or the 24-hour famine program. Or you might consider the programs of the Catholic Campaign for Human Development (CCHD). Make sure you include examples of direct outreach and education for justice. You can obtain information at the Catholic Relief Services and CCHD Web sites.
   - Put a face on outreach efforts by asking a teen or an adult to talk about his or her visit to a sister parish in an impoverished country or experiences on a recent mission trip.

2. Give each retreatant a copy of handout 15. Highlight the information on the right foot and make a connection to the examples of service you shared in the previous discussion.

Break (10:25 A.M.)

Catholic Social Teaching: A Call to Justice (10:55 A.M.)

Preparation

- Gather the following supplies:
  - ❑ newsprint
- Write each of the Catholic social teachings on a separate sheet of newsprint:
  - ❑ life and dignity of the human person
  - ❑ call to family, community, and participation
  - ❑ rights and responsibilities
  - ❑ option for the poor and the vulnerable
  - ❑ the dignity of work and the rights of the workers
  - ❑ solidarity
  - ❑ care for God's creation
- Post the sheets of newsprint in visible locations throughout the room.

1. Begin this activity by asking retreatants to return to the handout they received in the last activity, "The Two Feet of Christian Service." Then offer the following comments:

   In our last activity, we explored a bit what it means to be following in the footsteps of Jesus, living the Gospel message to love one another. But we are only standing on one foot. If we truly want to make a difference, we need to serve others and look for the root of the problem and ways to make a change at the root. The Catholic Church has a rich treasure of teachings on social justice.

   Catholic social teaching begins with the belief that we are all created in the image and likeness of God. Therefore, each person must be treated with respect and dignity. Our Catholic faith demands that we live out the Gospel by ensuring the rights of each person. The Church asks to follow Catholic social teaching when we work for the common good of all.

2. Referring to the listings you have noted on the newsprint, review each of the Catholic social teachings:

   Life and Dignity of the Human Person: The Catholic Church proclaims that all human life is sacred and values the dignity of every human person.

   Call to Family, Community, and Participation: We believe people have a right to participate in society, working together for the common good, especially the poor and vulnerable.

   Rights and Responsibilities: To protect human dignity, human rights must be respected and responsibilities met. We have a responsibility to one another, our families, and the larger society.

   Option for the Poor and the Vulnerable: The Gospel of Jesus Christ requires us to put the needs of the poor and vulnerable first.

The Dignity of Work and the Rights of the Workers: The basic rights of workers must be respected. Work is more than a way to make a living.

Solidarity: We are one human family. Loving our neighbor has global dimensions. The Gospel calls us to be peacemakers.

Care for God's Creation: We show our respect for God in how we care for the earth. We are called to protect people and the planet.

(*Note*: The Publishing Division of the United States Conference of Catholic Bishops has a wonderful two-sided color card that gives a more detailed summary of each of the Catholic social teachings.)

3. Ask each group to choose one of the Catholic social teachings. Using handout 15, ask them to list examples for both feet. Allow about 10 minutes for this activity.

4. Gather in a large group and invite a spokesperson from each small group to share the results of the discussion. Close by encouraging the retreatants to continue this conversation when they return to the parish and school and plan future outreach efforts.

Why I Am a Catholic: Talk 2 (11:40 A.M.)

Preparation

- Ask a newly confirmed Catholic, a young adult who has moved from the faith of his or her parents to confirming his or her own faith, to prepare a 15-minute talk on why he or she is Catholic. To help the person prepare, give him or her a copy of resource 14, "Suggestions for the Why I Am a Catholic Talk," as well as a copy of appendix A, "Helpful Hints for Giving Talks."

1. Introduce the team member giving this talk.

2. After the talk, allow 5 minutes for reflection and journal writing.

Saints and Sinners (12:00 P.M.)

Preparation

- Choose a sung refrain for praying the Litany of the Saints. "Litany of the Saints," by John D. Becker (OCP Publications, 1987) is especially nice and easy to learn. A variety of litanies can be found in almost every parish hymnal or songbook.
- Recruit a team member to serve as the music leader. This person will need to become familiar with the song you have selected.

1. Introduce this prayer in the following way:

> A *litany* is a form of prayer in which a prayer leader says a prayer and a group of people say or sing a response. There are many litanies in the Catholic tradition, but the Litany of the Saints is one of the oldest. The prayer is sung at Easter Vigil, on All Saints Day, and at ordinations. As Catholics, we believe in the communion of the saints. We call on the saints to intercede to Jesus for our needs and concerns.

2. Invite the designated prayer leader to come forward and lead the participants in the litany.

Lunch (12:30 P.M.)

Name That Sacrament (1:15 P.M.)

Preparation

- Gather the following supplies:
  - ❑ newsprint and markers
  - ❑ index cards
- Create a deck of cards by writing the following terms associated with sacraments on cards, one word or phrase per card:
  - ❑ Baptism: water, candle, white garment, new life, welcome, chrism
  - ❑ Reconciliation: sins, confession, absolution, penance, act of contrition, forgiveness
  - ❑ Eucharist: bread, wine, body, blood, chalice, Mass, sacrifice, thanksgiving, Jesus Christ
  - ❑ Confirmation: chrism, bishop, Holy Spirit, Pentecost, gifts of spirit, laying on of hands
  - ❑ Matrimony: rings, bride, groom, vocation, unity, vows
  - ❑ Holy Orders: chrism, stole, priest, vocation, bishop, laying on of hands
  - ❑ Anointing of the Sick: prayer, oil of the sick, health, sickness, dying, healing

1. Combine the small groups to create two or three teams and invite the retreatants to play this version of *Pictionary* or *Win, Lose, or Draw*. Provide the teams with the following instructions:

   The first team will choose someone to draw first. That person will pick a card and quickly draw an image on newsprint to represent the word or phrase on the card. Numbers, letters, and words cannot be used, and the person drawing is not allowed to speak.

   The first team has one minute to guess the word and the sacrament it represents. If the group is unable to guess the word and sacrament, any of the other groups may try.

   We will repeat the process for each card, rotating the groups with each turn.

2. Clarify any questions the groups might have and proceed with the game in the time allotted.

(This activity is adapted from Maryann Hakowski, *Vine and Branches 1*, pp. 40–41.)

We Are an Easter People; We Are a Sacramental People (1:45 P.M.)

Preparation

- Gather the following supplies:
  - ❑ three or more kinds of eggs (e.g., a plastic Easter egg, a ceramic or finely decorated Easter egg, and a regular chicken egg)
  - ❑ an Easter candle or a large white pillar candle and a stand
  - ❑ a taper candle

1. Introduce this prayer point in the following way:
   (*Hold up the eggs you have brought with you and pass them around the group, if possible.*)

   Easter eggs are dyed and shared and sometimes even turned into egg salad. They are filled with candy and hidden. They are made in chocolate molds and gelatin molds. But what is so "Easter" about an egg? Perhaps it is the promise of new life, of life in Christ. Perhaps the three parts of an egg—yolk, white, and shell—remind us of the Trinity. Perhaps we want to break out of the darkness inside our own shells and see the light, see the light of Christ.

2. Proclaim John 20:1–18. Allow a few moments of silence following the proclamation.

3. Gather the retreatants around the Easter candle and offer the following comments:

   At the very start of the Easter Vigil, the greatest celebration of the Church year, the community waits in darkness. As the first light of Easter appears, the deacon sings, "Christ our light." And we sing, "Thanks be to God" (*Sacramentary*, p. 173). The people who lived in darkness have seen a great light. Jesus has died and risen from the dead. He is our salvation.

Easter and the Easter season are the primary focus of the liturgical year. Easter celebrates the wonder and joy of Christ's Resurrection, the central mystery of our faith. It is a time of joy and hope, for death has been overcome and Christ has made us all heirs to the Kingdom of God. Because of the events of Easter, we dare to hope for our own Resurrection and eternal life with God.

4. Conclude with the following:

Christ has risen. Alleluia. Alleluia.

Invite all to respond, "Thanks be to God: Alleluia. Alleluia."

Why I Am a Catholic: Talk 3 (1:55 P.M.)

Preparation

- Ask a convert who has recently participated in the Rite of Christian Initiation of Adults (RCIA) program to prepare a 15-minute talk on why he or she is Catholic. To help the person prepare, give him or her a copy of resource 14, "Suggestions for the Why I Am a Catholic Talk," as well as a copy of appendix A, "Helpful Hints for Giving Talks."

1. Introduce the team member giving this talk.

2. After the talk, allow 5 minutes for quiet reflection and journal writing.

Signs and Wonders (2:15 P.M.)

Preparation

- Gather the following supplies:
  - ❑ a baptismal candle
  - ❑ chrism oil (just for viewing). If you do not have access to chrism oil, a perfumed oil is fine, as well.
  - ❑ a white garment
  - ❑ seven copies of *The Catholic Youth Bible* or another Bible
  - ❑ a large white pillar candle
  - ❑ a purple stole
  - ❑ a loaf of bread (not sandwich bread)
  - ❑ a chalice
  - ❑ a paten
  - ❑ a red cloth
  - ❑ a set of wedding rings
  - ❑ oil of the sick (just for viewing.) If you do not have access to the oil of the sick, a perfumed oil is fine.
  - ❑ a pyx

- ❑ hymnals or songbooks that include "Who Calls You by Name," by David Haas, or another song on the theme of being called
- ❑ copies of resource 16, "Called by Name," one for each prayer leader and cantor

- Place symbols at each of the seven sites, as indicated on resource 16.
- Ask two team members, one teen and one adult, to lead the prayer at each stop. Provide each with a copy of resource 16.
- Ask seven teens to prepare for and proclaim the Scripture readings. Provide each with a copy of resource 16 and a Bible.
- Ask a musical team member to serve as the cantor and teach the group the refrain of "Who Calls You by Name" or the alternative song you have selected.

1. Proceed with the prayer service as found on resource 16.

Free Time (3:00 P.M.)

The Spirit Moves Us: The Call of Pentecost (4:15 P.M.)

Preparation

- Gather the following supplies:
  - ❑ a large lock from a door (If you cannot locate one, start this activity in a room that has a door with a lock.)
  - ❑ *The Catholic Youth Bible* or another Bible

1. Introduce this prayer point in the following way:
   (*Hold up the lock. If you are in a room with several visible doors, get the group's attention by walking around and locking all the doors.*)

   After the Resurrection, after Jesus ascended into heaven, he appeared to the disciples several times. Thomas even put his hands in the wounds of Jesus so he would believe. And how did the disciples respond to the Resurrection of Jesus? They hid in a room. They locked the doors. They were not going anywhere.

2. Proclaim Acts 2:1–4. Allow a few moments of silence following the proclamation.

3. Continue with these comments:

   Pentecost is part of the Easter season and occurs approximately fifty days after Easter. It is often called the birthday of the Church, for on this day the Holy Spirit gave the Apostles courage to preach the Gospel of Jesus Christ. The celebration marks the formal end of the Easter season, just as these last few hours will mark the end of our retreat. So, what are you going to do with what you learned at this retreat? Are you going to go home and lock yourself up in your room?

   Let us pray that all of us will carry with us the same kind of courage as the disciples, so that we can go forth to share the Good News of our faith with others. Let us pray:

> Come, Holy Spirit. Fill the hearts of your faithful. Enkindle in them the fire of your love. Send forth your Spirit, and they will be created. And you will renew the face of the earth.

Witness Wear (4:30 P.M.)

Preparation

- Gather the following supplies:
  - ❑ two sheets of newsprint for each group
  - ❑ markers
- Make all the coloring materials available on a large supply table.

1. Introduce this activity in the following way:

> There are many ways to share what we have learned during this retreat experience—that it is "Cool to Be Catholic." As the retreat winds down, we invite you to start a line of "witness wear" by designing a T-shirt that captures your pride in being Catholic. Some examples include "One Cool Catholic," "Being Catholic—The Real Thing," "I believe! I believe!" on the front of the shirt and "It's Cool to Be Catholic" on the back.

2. Distribute markers and two sheets of newsprint to each small group. Encourage the groups to be creative and use symbols or words, or both. They should design both the front and the back of a shirt. They can use the scrap paper to sketch out design possibilities before settling on one example for the group. Allow at least 30 minutes for them to design the shirt.

3. Invite each group to share its designs and the reasons for choosing certain words or images. Once each group has shared, offer your own closing thoughts and comments about the retreat experience.

Options: Allow each individual to design a shirt. Consider this the first step in designing a youth-group or class shirt. Another option is to provide the retreatants with T-shirts and fabric markers or paints so they can design the group T-shirt at the retreat.

(This activity is adapted from Maryann Hakowski, *Sharing the Sunday Scriptures with Youth*, *Cycle A*, p. 130.)

Dinner (5:30 P.M.)

Preparation for Liturgy (6:15 P.M.)

During this time, you may want to have retreatants pack up their personal items and do any clean-up that is necessary.

Closing Liturgy (7:00 P.M.)

Celebrate the liturgy with the retreatants and, if you so choose, other parish members such as family and friends. Before the recessional song, it would be appropriate to thank the team and encourage the retreatants to continue celebrating their faith and living what they have learned and experienced during the retreat.

Alternative Ideas for This Retreat

Here are some activity ideas that can be used for a longer version of this retreat or as alternative activities:

- Include a "Breaking Open the Word" activity, using the Scripture passages for the upcoming weekend liturgies or following the lectionary. Or give each group a Scripture passage about discipleship and ask them to discuss how Jesus is calling them and how they might respond. Some possibilities are Matthew 4:18–22, 28:16–20; Mark 6:6–12; Luke 5:27–32, 14:25–33; and John 15:1–8.
- If you are not able to celebrate Mass, consider using the "Signs and Wonders" prayer as your closing prayer. Consider attending Mass together as a group after returning to the parish on Sunday.
- If the retreat takes place during Lent, replace the "Praying the Rosary" night prayer with praying the stations of the cross. Involve the retreatants in the stations by allowing them to (a) act on the stations with drama, or (b) create freeze-frame silent stations (shadow stations) or silhouettes behind a sheet lighted from the back. If you use a published stations of the cross booklet for teens, invite the retreatants to walk as they pray and take turns with the readings and prayers.

Resource 12

Suggestions for the Welcome and Opening Talk

This talk introduces the theme of the retreat, "It's Cool to Be Catholic," to the retreatants and prepares them for what they are going to experience. You have about 20 minutes for this presentation. The following outline provides ideas and thought starters.

Let's Hear It for God

- We take pride in who we are and where we belong. We cheer for our favorite sports team, we cheer for our favorite political candidate, and we put bumper stickers on our cars and wear team jerseys.
- Ask someone to share his or her high school cheer or school song. Offer your own cheer or sing your own song.
- This retreat is a chance to cheer for God, to take pride in our faith and our Church, and to recognize God's many blessings and share them.

So What's So Cool About Being Catholic?

- We are a sacramental people. We are a Eucharistic people. We are rooted in the Scriptures.
- We are part of a parish church, a diocesan church, and the universal, worldwide Church.
- At any moment at any time on any day, someone somewhere is celebrating Mass.

One, Holy, Catholic, Apostolic

- One: We believe in one Lord, one faith, one God in the Trinity. Though we are different, we are one.
- Holy: We all strive to be holy, to be united with God. But we are human; we are sinners. We strive to follow the example of the saints and grow closer to God.
- Catholic: We are universal. *Catholic* can be defined as "Here comes everybody," for everyone is welcome—all ages, races, nations, abilities, and so on. We are called by Christ and given a mission to share the Gospel with all and build the Reign of God.
- Apostolic: The leadership of our Church began with the Apostles and has been passed down to popes and bishops and priests through the laying on of hands. We are rooted in the Scriptures and the Catholic Tradition.

What to Expect at This Retreat

- A journey through the liturgical seasons of the Church.
- Catholic prayers, traditions, and devotions.
- The call to peace and justice.

- Sacramental signs and the wonders of grace.
- Breaking bread and breaking open the word of God.
- Sharing in the stories of faith of Catholic Christians.

Together on a Journey

- At this retreat, we will share in the faith journeys of several people who think it is very cool to be Catholic.
- We are not alone on this journey. We go with God and we go with others.
- Take time during the retreat to learn more about yourself, to make new friends, and to grow in your relationship with God.

Handout 12

Cool Bingo Questions

Self

- What is the coolest music you like to listen to?
- Name one cool gift or talent you like to share.
- What is cool about being you?
- When God created me, the coolest thing he made was . . .
- What cool movie have you seen lately?
- What is the coolest gift you have ever received?

Others

- Name one cool thing you like to do with your friends.
- Name one cool thing about your parents.
- The coolest thing about my best friend is . . .
- What is the coolest thing you have ever done on vacation with your family?
- Why is it cool to have a brother or a sister?

God

- The coolest thing about God's love is . . .
- Name one cool thing that Jesus did.
- Name one cool thing that Jesus said.
- It is cool to be Catholic because . . .
- It is cool to be on retreat because . . .

Handout 13

The Creed

We believe in one God,
the Father Almighty,
creator of heaven and earth,
of all that is seen and unseen.
We believe in one Lord, Jesus Christ,
the only Son of God,
eternally begotten of the Father,
God from God, Light from Light,
true God from true God,
begotten, not made, one in being with the Father.
Through him all things were made.
For us and our salvation
he came down from heaven;
by the power of the Holy Spirit
he was born of the Virgin Mary, and became man.
For our sake he was crucified under Pontius Pilate;
he suffered, died, and was buried.
On the third day he rose again
in fulfillment of the Scriptures;
he ascended into heaven
and is seated at the right hand of the Father.
He will come in glory to judge the living and the dead,
And his kingdom will have no end.
We believe in the Holy Spirit,
the Lord, the giver of life,
who proceeds from the Father and the Son.
He is worshiped and glorified
and has spoken through the prophets.
We believe in one holy catholic and apostolic Church.
We acknowledge one Baptism for the forgiveness of sins.
We look for the resurrection of the dead,
and the life of the world to come.
Amen.

Resource 13

Of Water and Light

Prayer Leader 1: During our last activity, we prayed and reflected on the creed, our statement of belief as Catholics. You gave wonderful, creative expression to your reflections. Now we gather as Catholic Christians to affirm this faith that we pray and accept anew every time we gather together at Mass.

Prayer Leader 2: When we were baptized, our parents and godparents gathered around a baptismal font. They spoke up for you and accepted your faith for you. Every time you pray the creed, you reclaim your faith. Every time we renew our baptismal promises, we reclaim our faith.

Tonight, we invite you to join together in renewing our baptismal promises.

Prayer Leader 3: Please respond by saying "I do" to the following questions:

Leader: Do you reject sin, so as to live in the freedom of God's children?
All: I do.

Leader: Do you reject the glamour of sin and refuse to be mastered by it?
All: I do.

Leader: Do you reject Satan, father of sin and prince of darkness?
All: I do.

Leader: Do you believe in God, the Father Almighty, creator of heaven and earth?
All: I do.

Leader: Do you believe in Jesus Christ, his only Son, our Lord, who was born of the Virgin Mary, was crucified, died, and was buried, rose from the dead, and is now seated at the right hand of the Father?
All: I do.

Leader: Do you believe in the Holy Spirit, the holy catholic Church, the communion of saints, the forgiveness of sins, the resurrection of the body, and life everlasting?
All: I do.

Leader: This is our faith. This is the faith of the Church. We are proud to profess it, in Christ Jesus our Lord.
All: Amen.

(Adapted from the "Renewal of Baptismal Promises," in the *Sacramentary*, pp. 204–205)

Prayer Leader 1: We will now listen to a song called "Creed," by Third Day (*or the alternate song you have chosen*). Just as we shared what the creed meant to us in a variety of ways, this Christian group has set the creed to music in a powerful prayer.

Prayer Leader 2: As you listen to the song, we invite you, one at a time, to dip your hand into the water and make the sign of the cross. After you do this, please come forward and light a candle from the Easter candle as a sign of your willingness to try to live the faith that you profess.

(*Cue song.*)

(*When all have blessed themselves and lit their candles, invite them to process silently in single file out of the chapel or retreat prayer space.*)

Resource 14

Suggestions for the Why I Am a Catholic Talk (Talks 1, 2, and 3)

This talk is one of three that allows retreatants to hear the faith stories of fellow Catholics who are excited by and committed to their faith. You have about 20 minutes for this presentation. The following outline provides ideas and thought starters.

Why Are You a Catholic?

- Why did you decide to become a Catholic? Why did you decide to stay a Catholic?
- Share part of the personal story of your journey of faith.
- Share a Catholic tradition or devotion that is important to you.
- Share your favorite Scripture passage.

Companions on a Journey

- How have others had an impact on your faith journey?
- How have you touched the faith journey of others?
- How are you nourished, in body and spirit, when you attend Mass?

What Does It Mean to Live Your Faith?

- How does being Catholic influence your decisions?
- How do you share your faith in word and action?
- How are you involved in your community of faith?
- How do you share your gifts and talents?
- Give at least one reason why you believe it is "Cool to Be Catholic."
- Close with a challenge for the retreatants to continue learning and growing in faith.

Resource 15

A Living Rosary

Prayer Leader: Invite everyone to begin by making the sign of the cross.

Processional cross holder: I believe in God, the Father Almighty, creator of heaven and earth. I believe in Jesus Christ, his only Son, our Lord. He was conceived by the power of the Holy Spirit, and born of the Virgin Mary. He suffered under Pontius Pilate, was crucified, died, and was buried. He descended to the dead. On the third day he rose again. He ascended into heaven and is seated at the right hand of the Father. He will come again to judge the living and the dead.

I believe in the Holy Spirit, the holy catholic Church, the communion of saints, the forgiveness of sins, the resurrection of the body, and life everlasting. Amen.

Red Candle Bearer 1: Our Father, who art in heaven, hallowed be thy name. Thy kingdom come. Thy will be done on earth, as it is in heaven.

All: Give us this day our daily bread, and forgive us our trespasses, as we forgive those who trespass against us, and lead us not into temptation, but deliver us from evil. Amen.

Blue Candle Bearer 1: Hail Mary, full of grace, the Lord is with you; blessed are you among women, and blessed is the fruit of your womb, Jesus.

All: Holy Mary, Mother of God, pray for us sinners now and at the hour of our death. Amen.

Prayer Leader: Glory be to the Father, and to the Son, and to the Holy Spirit,

All: As it was in the beginning, is now, and will be forever. Amen.

Prayer Leader: *Announce the first of the joyful mysteries, the Annunciation.*

Red Candle Bearer 2: Our Father, who art in heaven . . .

Blue Candle Bearer 2: Hail Mary, full of grace . . .

Blue Candle Bearer 3: Hail Mary, full of grace . . .

Blue Candle Bearer 4: Hail Mary, full of grace . . .

Blue Candle Bearer 5: Hail Mary, full of grace . . .

Prayer Leader: Glory be to the Father, and to the Son, and to the Holy Spirit,

All: As it was in the beginning, is now, and will be forever. Amen.

(*Continue in this fashion until you have completed all five decades, announcing each of the remaining joyful mysteries accordingly: The Visitation, The Birth of Our Lord, The Presentation of Jesus in the Temple, The Finding of Jesus in the Temple.*)

Handout 14

The Second Station of the Cross: Jesus Is Made to Take Up His Cross

Leader: Saving and forgiving Lord, we love you, we need you, and we trust you.

All: Give us the strength to follow your way of living and loving.

Leader: Lord, Jesus, you did not ask for your cross, yet you picked it up. You did not ask to be mistreated, yet you accepted mistreatment rather than abandon your commitment to nonviolence and unconditional love. Where did you get your strength? Your heart must have been so heavy with sadness, your body so sore from being beaten, your spirit so weak as you wondered why this violence was being done to you.

All: Forgive me, Lord, for the times I take the easy way out. Forgive me for the times I choose to use violent words or actions rather than take up my cross and suffer for the sake of love. To be honest, Lord, I am afraid to take up my cross. I am not sure what it means. I think you are telling me to face the pain in my life, to let go of revenge and forgive someone who has hurt me, to let go of the fear of befriending someone who is lonely or left out, to deal with my personal problems with courage.

Silent reflection. What are your crosses? That is, what challenging or difficult situations are you facing?

All: Jesus, by the power of your spirit, who lives within each of us, help us to trust in your promise to be with us always as we take up our crosses. During our roughest and most challenging times, help us to lean on you and support one another. Remind us of how near you are and how eager you are to help us cope with the pain we each face. Teach us to love. Amen.

(Taken from Gary Egeberg, *Stations for Teens: Meditations on the Death and Resurrection of Jesus* [Winona, MN: Saint Mary's Press, 1999], page 13.

Handout 15

The Two Feet of Christian Service

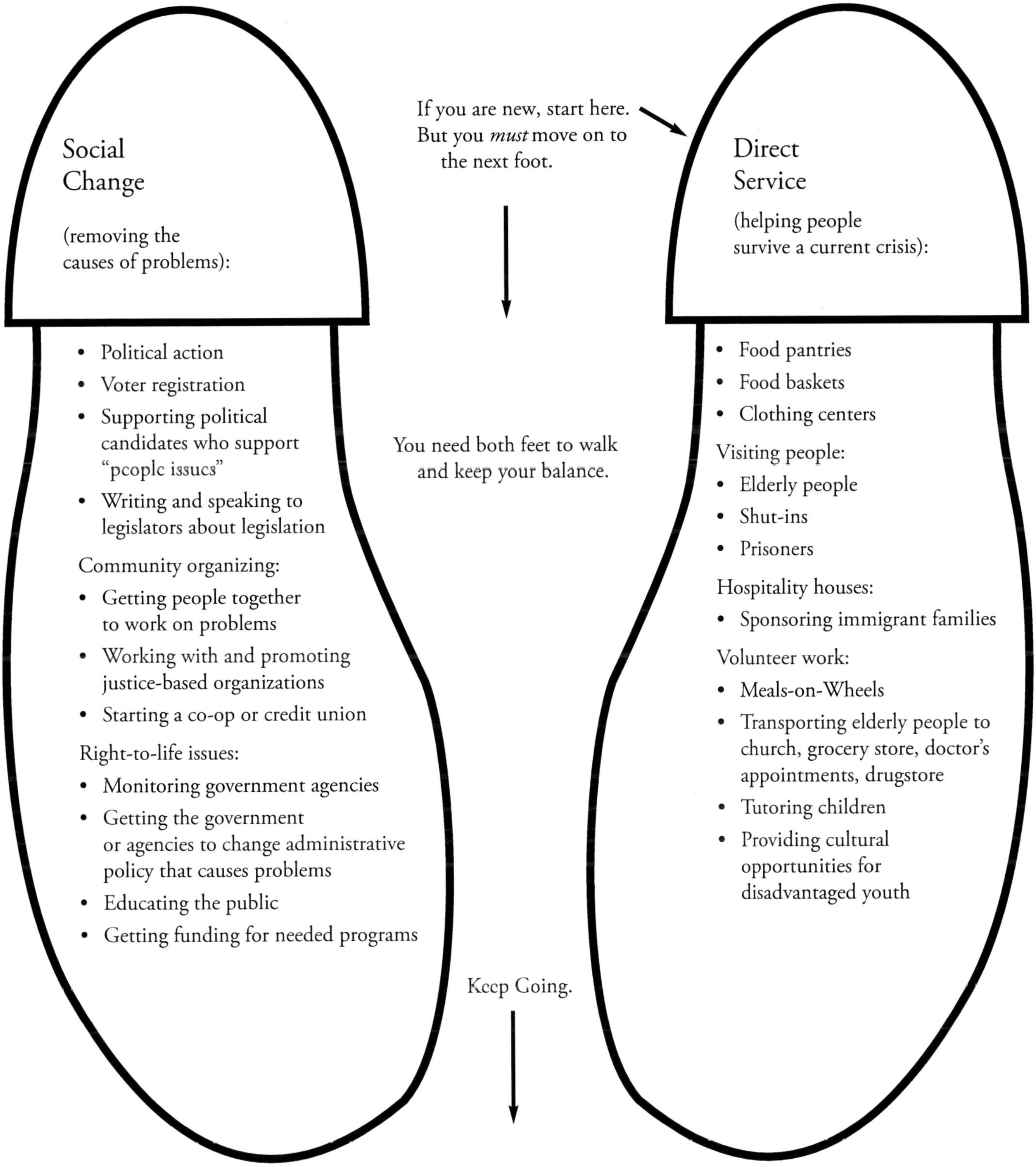

If you are new, start here. But you *must* move on to the next foot.

You need both feet to walk and keep your balance.

Keep Going.

Social Change

(removing the causes of problems):

- Political action
- Voter registration
- Supporting political candidates who support "people issues"
- Writing and speaking to legislators about legislation

Community organizing:

- Getting people together to work on problems
- Working with and promoting justice-based organizations
- Starting a co-op or credit union

Right-to-life issues:

- Monitoring government agencies
- Getting the government or agencies to change administrative policy that causes problems
- Educating the public
- Getting funding for needed programs

Direct Service

(helping people survive a current crisis):

- Food pantries
- Food baskets
- Clothing centers

Visiting people:

- Elderly people
- Shut-ins
- Prisoners

Hospitality houses:

- Sponsoring immigrant families

Volunteer work:

- Meals-on-Wheels
- Transporting elderly people to church, grocery store, doctor's appointments, drugstore
- Tutoring children
- Providing cultural opportunities for disadvantaged youth

(Adapted from a study sheet in *Poverty and FaithJustice*, by the Campaign for Human Development [Washington, DC: United States Conference of Catholic Bishops (USCCB), 1998], page 20. Copyright © 1998 by the USCCB, Inc. Used with permission.)

Resource 16

Called by Name

Baptism

(*Lead the group to the baptismal font or a clear bowl of water near the Easter candle or large candle, where you have placed a baptismal candle, chrism, and white garment.*)

(*All join in the refrain of the song.*)

Reader 1: Let us pray for all children who are baptized into our parish community that they and their parents continue to grow in faith. Our response will be: Fill us with your grace.

Reader 2: Let us pray for adults who take a leap of faith into our font and become part of our faith through the Sacrament of Baptism.

All: Fill us with your grace.

Reader 3: (*Proclaim Mark 1:9–11.*)

Reconciliation

(*Lead the group to the reconciliation room or confessional, where you have placed a candle and a purple stole.*)

(*All join in the refrain of the song.*)

Reader 1: Let us pray for those who are about to receive the sacrament of Penance and Reconciliation for the first time. May they experience the joy of God's great gift of forgiveness.

All: Fill us with your grace.

Reader 2: Let us pray for all those who are separated by sin from God and others, that they find the courage to receive the sacrament of Penance and Reconciliation.

All: Fill us with your grace.

Reader 4: (*Proclaim Matthew 18:21–22.*)

Eucharist

(*Invite the group to the altar or prayer table, where you have placed a loaf of bread, a chalice, and a paten.*)

(*All join in the refrain of the song.*)

Reader 1: Let us pray for all who will receive their first Eucharist this year, that they grow daily in the love of Christ.

All: Fill us with your grace.

Reader 2: Let us pray for our parish community, that we come often to the table of the Lord to be nourished in body and soul.

All: Fill us with your grace.

Reader 5: (*Proclaim Mark 14:22–25.*)

Confirmation

(*Return to the baptismal font near the Easter candle; a team member has draped a red cloth near the white garment here.*)

(*All join in the refrain of the song.*)

Reader 1: Let us pray for all those preparing to receive the sacrament of Confirmation, that the Holy Spirit may guide and inspire and challenge them.

All: Fill us with your grace.

Reader 2: Let us pray for all who have been confirmed, that they are filled with the spirit of wisdom and understanding, the spirit of right judgment and courage, the spirit of knowledge and reverence, and the spirit of wonder and awe in God's presence.

All: Fill us with your grace.

Reader 6: (*Proclaim Acts 2:1–4.*)

Matrimony

(*Lead the group to a kneeler for two in front of the altar, where you have placed wedding rings and a set of unity candles.*)

(*All join in the refrain of the song.*)

Reader 1: Let us pray for all those who will be married at our parish this year, that they make Christ the center of their lives and grow in love and devotion to each other.

All: Fill us with your grace.

Reader 2: Let us pray for all those who are married, that they remain faithful to their wedding vows and bring Christ to life in their marriage.

All: Fill us with your grace.

Reader 7: (*Proclaim John 2:1–11.*)

Holy Orders

(*Lead the group to the ambo or the location in the prayer space where the Gospel is proclaimed and where you have placed a stole.*)

(*All join in the refrain of the song.*)

Reader 1: Let us pray for all young people in our parish, that they may be open to sharing their faith in a vocation as a priest, sister, brother, or lay minister.

All: Fill us with your grace.

Reader 2: Let us pray for all priests, that they do not lose heart as they share the Gospel, celebrate the Eucharist, and minister to God's people.

All: Fill us with your grace.

Reader 8: (*Proclaim Matthew 9:35–38.*)

Anointing of the Sick

(*Lead the group to a small table, where you have placed the oil of the sick, or other perfumed oil, and a pyx.*)

(*All join in the refrain of the song.*)

Reader 1: Let us pray for all those who suffer with illness, that God may grant them comfort in body and soul.

All: Fill us with your grace.

Reader 2: Let us pray for all those who have died, especially those who we hold dear, that they may find peace with Christ, who wipes away all our tears.

All: Fill us with your grace.

Reader 9: (*Proclaim Luke 18:35–43.*)

(*All join in the refrain of the song.*)

(Adapted from Maryann Hakowski, *22 Ready-Made Prayer Services with 100 Extra Prayer Ideas* [Winona, MN: Saint Mary's Press, 2006], pages 45–46.)

Retreat 5

Micah 6:8

Introduction

This weekend retreat uses the text of Micah 6:8 as a framework for weaving the Gospel values of humility, kindness, and love for justice into our way of thinking and way of life. Retreatants are also asked to follow Jesus's radical way of living for God and others.

Goals

- To build awareness of critical peace and justice concerns in our community and in our world.
- To build a sense of empathy and to encourage each retreatant to step outside of the comfort zone and walk in the shoes of another.
- To instill a sense of urgency about finding and addressing the roots of justice issues and developing action plans.
- To lift up the values of kindness and humility in our relationships with God and others.
- To learn how to weave a sense of justice and peace into our daily living and life's work.

Schedule

The following sequence for "Micah 6:8" is just one suggestion on how to arrange the schedule. Use the column labeled "Actual Plan" to record the activities, sequences, and starting times that will work for you.

Time	*Activity Name*	*Activity Type*	*Actual Plan*
Friday evening			
6:30 P.M.	Arrival		______
7:00 P.M.	Welcome and Journal Talk	Talk	______
7:20 P.M.	Micah 6:8	Theme talk	______
7:40 P.M.	Naming Our Gifts	Icebreaker	______
8:10 P.M.	Micah Quote Scavenger Hunt	Group forming	______
8:20 P.M.	Seeing the World Through Different Eyes	Prayer point	______
8:30 P.M.	Poverty Quiz	Discussion	______
9:00 P.M.	Snack Break		______
9:30 P.M.	Band-Aids and Crayons	Prayer point	______
9:40 P.M.	Passion for Justice Talk 1	Witness talk	______
10:00 P.M.	Newspapers and Justice	Activity	______
10:30 P.M.	Break		______
11:00 P.M.	Standing with Those Who Have Made a Difference	Night prayer	______
12:00 A.M.	Lights Out		______
Saturday			
7:45 A.M.	Rising		______
8:30 A.M.	Breakfast		______
9:00 A.M.	Walking in the Shoes of Another	Morning prayer	______
9:30 A.M.	Humility Charades	Community builder	______
9:50 A.M.	Coffee Filters and Faith	Prayer point	______
10:00 A.M.	Jesus and Justice	Witness talk	______
10:20 A.M.	What Does Jesus Teach Us About Justice?	Scripture activity	______
10:50 A.M.	Break		______
11:20 A.M.	Where Are Your Clothes Made?	Prayer point	______
11:30 A.M.	Passion for Justice Talk 2	Witness talk	______
11:50 A.M.	Justice *Jenga*	Activity and discussion	______
12:30 P.M.	Lunch		______

1:30 P.M.	A Card Game Called *Peace*	Prayer point	________
1:40 P.M.	If You Want Peace, Work for Justice	Video	________
2:10 P.M.	Footprints, Fingerprints, and Friendships	Activity	________
3:00 P.M.	Break		________
3:20 P.M.	Passion for Justice Talk 3	Witness talk	________
3:40 P.M.	Beatitudes for Living	Quiet reflection	________
4:00 P.M.	Free Time		________
5:30 P.M.	Dinner		________
6:30 P.M.	What Is Your Kindness Quotient?	Activity	________
7:00 P.M.	Forming the Justice League	Activity	________
8:00 P.M.	Break		________
8:30 P.M.	Passion for Justice Talk 4	Witness talk	________
8:50 P.M.	TV Shows and Justice	Activity	________
9:30 P.M.	Snack and Free Time		________
10:30 P.M.	A Season for Nonviolence	Night prayer	________
12:00 A.M.	Lights Out		________
Sunday			
7:45 A.M.	Rising		________
8:30 A.M.	Breakfast		________
9:00 A.M.	If We Are the Body, Why Aren't Our Hands Reaching?	Morning prayer	________
9:30 A.M.	Passion for Justice Talk 5	Witness talk	________
9:50 A.M.	The Baby That Floated Downstream	Prayer point	________
10:00 A.M.	Action Keys	Activity	________
10:45 A.M.	Break		________
11:00 A.M.	*Finding Nemo*, Swimming Down	Prayer point	________
11:10 A.M.	Be the Change You Want to See in the World	Wrap-up talk	________
11:30 A.M.	Weaving Justice	Craft	________
12:15 P.M.	Lunch		________
1:00 P.M.	Preparation for Liturgy		________
1:45 P.M.	Closing Liturgy		________

General Materials and Preparation

- The suggested space needs for this retreat include a large gathering space, tables for small groups, and a designated prayer space.
- Create a portable supply basket for each small group, containing the following frequently used items:
  - ❑ pens or pencils
  - ❑ markers
  - ❑ scissors
  - ❑ glue sticks
  - ❑ self-stick notes
  - ❑ participant journals
  - ❑ songbooks or hymnals
  - ❑ copies of *The Catholic Youth Bible* or another Bible

Detailed Description of Activities for Friday

Welcome and Journal Talk (7:00 P.M.)

Preparation

- Gather the following supplies:
  - ❑ spiral-bound notebooks or journals, one for each person
- Ask a young person on the team to prepare a 10-minute opening talk to welcome participants to the retreat. To help the person prepare, give her or him resource 17, "Suggestions for the Welcome and Opening Talk," as well as a copy of appendix A, "Helpful Hints for Giving Talks."

1. Welcome everyone to the retreat. Explain the ground rules and make announcements, if necessary. Introduce the team member who will be giving the welcome talk. Distribute the journals at the end of the talk.

Micah 6:8 (7:20 P.M.)

Preparation

- Ask a team member to prepare a 20-minute opening talk to introduce the theme of the retreat. To help the person prepare, give her or him a copy of resource 18, "Suggestions for the Micah 6:8 Talk," as well as a copy of appendix A, "Helpful Hints for Giving Talks."

1. Introduce the team member giving this talk.

2. After the talk, allow 5 minutes for reflection and journal writing.

Naming Our Gifts (7:40 P.M.)

Preparation

- Gather the following supplies:
  - ❑ small index cards, one for each retreatant

1. Distribute an index card to each person. Ask the retreatants to do the following:

   > In the center of the card, write the name of a hero, a leader, someone you admire. It could be a national or international figure, living or dead. It could be a teacher, coach, or parent who has really made a difference in the lives of others.

   Allow a few moments for them to complete this task, and then proceed with these instructions:

   > Around the name, write some of the qualities, gifts, or talents you admire in that person.

2. Ask the retreatants to move around the room, introduce themselves to several people, and tell them the name of the hero and his or her qualities noted on the card. The retreatants should be able to meet quite a few people during the 5-minute period.

3. Ask the participants to be seated. Then ask them to flip the index cards over. Each person can write her or his own name in the center of the card.

4. Invite people to write some of their own gifts, talents, and positive qualities on the card.

5. Once again, ask the retreatants to move around the room for about 5 minutes, introduce themselves to different people, and tell about some of their own positive qualities.

6. Close this activity by stressing that this retreat is a great opportunity to meet new people. It is also a great chance to learn more about people who have done some ordinary and extraordinary things to make a difference in our world. Affirm that each person at the retreat has a lot to offer, and encourage the retreatants to let their gifts and talents shine during the weekend.

Micah Quote Scavenger Hunt (8:10 P.M.)

Preparation

- Gather the following supplies:
  - ❑ small posters on which Micah 6:8 is written, one for each small group (each group poster should be a different color)
  - ❑ cellophane tape
- Create one Micah 6:8 poster for each group. Each poster should read: "What does the Lord require of you, but to do justice, and to love kindness, and to walk humbly with your God?"
- Before the retreat, divide the large group into small groups of seven or eight people. Write the name of each group member on the back of the group's poster. Each poster should be a different color. Cut each poster into seven or eight pieces, with one person's name on each piece.
- Before the retreatants arrive, hide the puzzle pieces.

1. Invite the retreatants to search around the room and find a puzzle piece. When everyone has found a puzzle piece, invite them to:

- look for the person whose name is on the puzzle piece
- introduce themselves to that person
- give the person the puzzle piece
- search for their own puzzle piece

Tell the retreatants that when they have found the person whose name is on the puzzle piece and when they have gotten their own puzzle pieces, they can sit down. Be sure that everyone has accomplished these tasks before moving on to the next step.

2. Ask the retreatants to find the other people holding puzzle pieces of the same color. Each color-coded group can find a table, sit down, and put their puzzle together.

3. Let the retreatants know that the groups they are in will be their small groups throughout the retreat.

Seeing the World Through Different Eyes (8:20 P.M.)

Preparation

- Gather the following supplies:
  - ❑ kaleidoscopes, one for each small group (small, inexpensive ones are fine)
  - ❑ songbooks with "We Are Called," by David Haas (1988, GIA Publications,) included. Or choose another song that goes with the retreat theme of Micah 6:8.

1. Distribute the kaleidoscopes. Invite one retreatant in each group to look through the kaleidoscope, describe what he or she sees inside, and then pass the kaleidoscope along to the next person in the group. Allow time for each group member to look through the kaleidoscope.

2. Pose the following questions, inviting a few responses for each:

- What is the difference between what you see when you look through the kaleidoscope and what you see when you are not looking through it?
- What did you have to do to make the pattern change inside the kaleidoscope?
- What did you notice as you listened to each person describe what they saw inside?
- What can we learn about peace and justice from this activity?

3. Summarize the answers, and continue with these comments:

> We are all different, and we look at different issues in different ways. We need to be willing to look at issues and problems in the world if we really want to live the Gospel message of Jesus Christ. We have the power to change the patterns of injustice around us.

4. Invite everyone to open their songbooks and join in singing the refrain to "We Are Called" or the song you have selected.

Poverty Quiz (8:30 P.M.)

Preparation

- Gather the following supplies:
  - ❑ copies of handout 16, "World Awareness Quiz," one for each retreatant
  - ❑ copies of handout 17, "World Awareness Quiz Answers," one for each small group

1. Introduce this activity in the following way:

> During this activity, you will take a quiz to see how aware you are of the needs of poor people in our world. The quiz will also help you contrast the needs of others with the wealth of resources we have as individuals and as a nation.

2. Give each person a copy of handout 16. Ask the retreatants to complete the quiz individually in silence. Allow enough time for everyone to complete the quiz.

3. Give each group a copy of handout 17. Allow time for the retreatants to mark the correct answers on their handouts.

4. Ask the retreatants to discuss these questions in their small groups:

- How did you do on the quiz?
- What did you learn from taking the quiz?
- How are you challenged by this discussion?

5. Close by encouraging the retreatants to learn more about these and other peace and justice issues. Encourage them to be open to new ideas and new ways of looking at issues. This quiz is just a start. Tell the group that as the retreat continues, they will look more deeply into several issues and put faces on some of the statistics.

Snack Break (9:00 P.M.)

Band-Aids and Crayons (9:30 P.M.)

Preparation

- Gather the following supplies:
  - ❑ 16-packs or 24-packs of crayons, one for each group
  - ❑ plain Band-Aids, one for each person

1. Place some Band-Aids and crayons on each table. Watch for a few minutes to see what people do with them. Do they unwrap the Band-Aids? Do they doodle with the crayons? Do they ask for permission to use them? Do they ask what they are for?

2. After a few moments have passed, pose the following questions:

- What do you do with a Band-Aid?
- What do you do with a crayon?
- How can a Band-Aid help us learn about peace and justice issues?
- How can a crayon be a tool for making a difference?

3. Summarize their answers, and continue with these comments:

> We need to be creative when we approach social justice issues. We have to find new uses for old tools and new approaches to old problems.
>
> We cannot wait for others to tell us what to do; we need to take some initiative and be leaders in our own ways. We also need to have the courage to color outside the lines, and that can be the toughest part of all.
>
> During the rest of the retreat, keep a crayon with you as a reminder of the need to be creative in solving problems and to have courage to color outside the lines when necessary. Put the Band-Aid on where it will be visible to you, as a reminder of the people throughout the world who are hurting.

4. Invite the retreatants to open their songbooks to "We Are Called," or the alternative song you have selected, and join in singing the refrain.

Passion for Justice Talk 1 (9:40 P.M.)

Preparation

- Ask a team member to reflect on one social justice issue and prepare a 15-minute talk. To help the person prepare, give him or her a copy of resource 19, "Suggestions for the Passion for Justice Talk," as well as a copy of appendix A, "Helpful Hints for Giving Talks."

1. Introduce the team member giving this talk.

2. After the talk, allow 5 minutes for quiet reflection and journal writing.

Newspapers and Justice (10:00 P.M.)

Preparation

- Gather the following supplies:
  - ❑ Prior to the retreat, clip articles from local newspapers that are related in some way to a social justice issue. Make sure you have a mix of local, national, and world articles. You should have at least five articles for each small group.
  - ❑ a sheet of newsprint (optional)

1. Introduce this activity in the following way:

   So far, we have heard a few talks, taken a quiz, and spent time getting to know one another better. Now we will start identifying some of the many social justice issues we face in the world today.

2. Distribute a few articles to each small group. Invite the groups to look over their articles for about 5 minutes and list on a blank sheet of paper the social justice issues found in them.

3. Next, ask them to choose one article to look at in depth. They can either pass it around or one person can read it aloud so everyone in the group is familiar with it.

4. Ask them to answer the following questions about that one article:

- What is the issue?
- What have you learned?
- How might we respond?
- What Scripture connection can you make with this issue?

Allow 15 minutes for them to complete this task.

5. Ask each group to choose a spokesperson to share the group's answers with the larger group. You may want to list all the issues on a sheet of newsprint.

6. Close this activity by encouraging the retreatants to become more aware of social justice issues, through newspapers and the other media. The first step in making a difference is to become aware of the challenges. Let them know that they will be touching on many of these issues again during the retreat.

Break (10:30 P.M.)

Standing with Those Who Have Made a Difference (11:00 P.M.)

Preparation

- Gather the following supplies:
  - ❑ a pillar candle
  - ❑ seven copies of resource 20, "Standing with Others Who Have Made a Difference"
- Recruit seven team members to serve as readers. Provide each with a copy of resource 20.

1. Invite the retreatants to join you in the prayer space and sit on the floor in a circle. Light the candle. Proceed with the prayer service as outlined on resource 20.

Lights Out (12:00 A.M.)

Detailed Description of Activities for Saturday

Rising (7:45 A.M.)

Breakfast (8:30 A.M.)

Walking in the Shoes of Another (9:00 A.M.)

Preparation

- Gather the following supplies:
  - ❑ pillar candles, one for each small group
  - ❑ songbooks that include "The Summons," by Kelvingrove (G.I.A. Publications, 1987), or another song with the theme of service
  - ❑ small safety pins, one for each person
  - ❑ construction paper
  - ❑ nine copies of resource 21, "Walking in Another's Shoes"
  - ❑ a CD of reflective instrumental music
  - ❑ a CD player
- Using construction paper and safety pins, create name tags in the shape of a shoe, one for each person
- Recruit eight team members to serve as readers of the prayer. Provide each with a copy of resource 21.
- Place the songbooks in the prayer space.

1. Invite the retreatants to join you in the prayer space. Ask them to remove their shoes before entering. Provide each with a songbook as they enter the space. Then ask that they sit in a circle with the other members of their group. Play some quiet instrumental music while they are getting situated. Proceed with the prayer service as noted on resource 21.

Note: Be sure to return the songbooks to the group tables.

Humility Charades (9:30 A.M.)

Preparation

- Gather the following supplies:
  - ❑ index cards, ten for each small group
  - ❑ a small basket

1. Give each small group ten index cards. Ask the retreatants in each group to write down five words that describe humility and five words that describe the opposite of humility. They should write one word on each card. Allow a few minutes for them to complete this task.

2. Collect all the cards and review them quickly, taking out any duplicates. Once you have sorted the cards, place them in a basket.

3. Ask a volunteer from each group to come forward and choose a card. Each person should act out the word on the card without using any words or making any sounds (as in Charades). Act out one word at a time. Ask the members of the audience to raise their hands and guess what word is being acted out.

4. Close this activity by inviting everyone to participate fully in all of the day's activities. Challenge them to look for ways they can "walk more humbly with their God."

Coffee Filters and Faith (9:50 A.M.)

Preparation

- Gather the following supplies:
  - ❑ large coffee filters, one for each small group

1. Give each small group a large coffee filter. Ask the groups to brainstorm at least twenty possible uses for the filters other than making coffee. Allow about 5 minutes for this activity.

2. Invite a spokesperson from each group to share their answers with the large group.

3. Offer the following comments:

   As Catholic Christians, we need to filter all we do and say through the life of Jesus Christ, through his Gospel message. Only then can we begin to model our own lives after his. If we use the life of Jesus as a filter—rather than using the societal filters of the media and celebrity—we are likely to be quite surprised and challenged by the results.

   The message of Jesus Christ was radical for his time, especially his championship of the poor and the vulnerable. His message continues to be radical in our time. Still today, despite all the advances in medicine and technology, the poor and the vulnerable rarely have a voice. They still need a champion in Jesus, and we are the ones to take up such causes.

   We will need to be very creative in how we answer the call to justice. Sometimes we will have to accomplish great things with very little. Just as we found, in our creative activity, that a simple coffee filter can have many uses, we too have many uses and are capable of making a greater difference than we imagine.

4. Conclude the activity by inviting the retreatants to join in singing the refrain to "We Are Called," or the alternative song you have selected.

Jesus and Justice (10:00 A.M.)

Preparation

- Ask a team member to prepare a 15-minute talk on Jesus and Justice. To help the person prepare, give him or her a copy of resource 22, "Suggestions for the Jesus and Justice Talk," as well as a copy of appendix A, "Helpful Hints for Giving Talks."

1. Introduce the team member giving this talk.

2. After the talk, allow 5 minutes for quiet reflection and journal writing.

What Does Jesus Teach Us About Justice? (10:20 A.M.)

Preparation

- Gather the following supplies:
  - ❑ newsprint
  - ❑ markers
- Write the following Scripture citations on newsprint and place them where all are able to see them:

❑ Luke 10:30–37	❑ Luke 12:13–21
❑ Matthew 14:13–21	❑ Matthew 5:1–12
❑ Mark 7:31–37	❑ Luke 15:3–7
❑ Luke 14:13–14	❑ Luke 18:15–17
❑ Matthew 5:38–42	❑ Matthew 9:3–6
❑ Luke 22:47–53	❑ Luke 9:46–48
❑ Matthew 6:19–24	❑ Luke 14:7–12

1. Ask each individual to take a few minutes and read over some of the Scripture passages you have written on the newsprint. Then ask the small groups to choose one passage for further reflection.

2. Ask the small groups to answer the following questions:

- What can we learn from this Scripture passage?
- How does this Scripture passage call us to live?

Allow about 10 minutes for the discussion.

3. Now ask the groups to write a prayer based on their understanding of the Scripture passage, using their discussion as a guide. Allow about 10 minutes for them to complete this task.

4. If time permits, invite a spokesperson from each group to summarize the discussion and share the prayers. Close by asking the retreatants to take the examples from the life of Jesus and weave them into their own lives. Encourage them to turn to the Scriptures to find inspiration, challenges for daily living, and occasions for prayer.

Break (10:50 A.M.)

Where Are Your Clothes Made? (11:20 A.M.)

Preparation

- Gather the following supplies:
  - ❑ a map of the world
  - ❑ a bulletin board
  - ❑ colorful pushpins
- Attach the map to the bulletin board and place it where it can be easily seen by all.

1. Ask the retreatants to pair up and look at the clothing labels inside their shirts or jackets and find out where their clothes were made. Ask them to come forward and place a pushpin on the map to show the country where workers made the clothes they are wearing today.

2. Then ask the following questions:

- Were you surprised when you found out where your clothes were made? Have you ever thought about this before?
- Where do you think most of our clothes, electronic equipment, and other consumer goods are made? Where does a lot of our food come from?
- Why do you think many companies outsource work to countries other than our own?
- What can it mean for people who make our goods in other countries, sometimes working in sweatshop conditions?

Invite several retreatants to share their thoughts on these questions.

3. Summarize the answers, and then continue with these comments:

> We are dependent on other countries for most of our clothes, food, and other goods. Some would say we are a consumer society.
>
> In our call toward justice, we need to learn more about where these goods are made and how the workers are treated by company managers and officers. We then must make some tough choices about what we buy and which companies we support when we make our purchases.
>
> This is a start in questioning systems that maximize profits by using poverty-stricken workers in other countries. If we take the time to learn about the issues and the people, we can begin to make a difference.

4. Conclude by inviting everyone to join in singing the refrain of "We Are Called," or the alternative song the group has been singing throughout the retreat.

Passion for Justice Talk 2 (11:30 A.M.)

Preparation

- Ask a team member to prepare a 15-minute talk on justice. To help the person prepare, give him or her a copy of resource 19, "Suggestions for the Passion for Justice Talk," as well as a copy of appendix A, "Helpful Hints for Giving Talks."

1. Introduce the team member giving this talk.

2. After the talk, allow 5 minutes for reflection and journal writing.

Justice *Jenga* (11:50 A.M.)

Preparation

- Gather the following supplies:
  - ❑ *Jenga* games (Milton Bradley Company), one for each small group
  - ❑ newsprint
  - ❑ markers
- Write each of the following words on one of the Jenga blocks:

❑ community participation	❑ health benefits
❑ work-owned business	❑ drug free
❑ community policing	❑ clean air
❑ home ownership	❑ clean water
❑ affordable rent	❑ healthy families
❑ access to education	❑ civic participation
❑ a functioning car	❑ affordable housing
❑ living wage	❑ physically able to work
❑ public transportation	❑ community activism
❑ safe environment	❑ adequate health care coverage

You will need to write these words on each set of blocks.

- Post the following questions on newsprint:
  - ❑ Why is it important for people to have ________________?
  - ❑ What happens to this community, to this society, if people do not have this necessity?
- Assemble a tower, using one set of blocks, on each of the small-group tables. Make sure that blocks with words are interspersed with plain blocks in the tower and are not all located in one place.

1. Ask the retreatants to be careful not to knock down or touch the tower you have created on each table. Invite the groups to play *Jenga* by carefully taking out one of the blocks and putting it on top of the tower.

If the block has a word on it, group members should answer the two questions you have posted on newsprint as they relate to that word.

Offer the following example:

- If your block says "affordable housing," your questions are:
  - Why is it so important for people to have affordable housing?
  - What happens when people cannot find affordable housing?

2. Tell the retreatants that if they take out a blank block, they simply "pass" on the discussion part of the game and allow the next person to play.

Allow each group to play the game until all or part of the *Jenga* tower falls down.

3. Invite some large-group discussion by posing these questions:

- What can this activity teach us about peace and justice issues?
- What happens to a society or community if the basic needs of even some of its citizens are not met?

Conclude with these comments:

> This activity shows us how the building blocks of society, which are the elements that fulfill the basic needs of individuals and families, must be available in order for society to survive. It can also help us recognize how we are all interconnected and how when some of us are lacking, many suffer.

Lunch (12:30 P.M.)

A Card Game Called *Peace* (1:30 P.M.)

Preparation

- Gather the following supplies:
  - ❑ two decks of playing cards for each small group

1. Give each small group two decks of playing cards and have someone shuffle the decks and deal all the cards to group members. Tell the retreatants that you are going to teach them how to play a new card game called *Peace*.

2. Give the following directions:

> Each person turns over a card. The person with the lowest number gets to keep all the cards in that round. (Aces count as 1 point; kings are the highest card.) If two people have the same card, each person places three cards face down and turns the fourth card up. Once again, the lowest card wins.
>
> If someone runs out of cards, the person with the most cards gives half of her or his cards to the person with none.

Make sure everyone understands the rules before inviting the small groups to play. Let the groups play the game for a few minutes.

3. Invite the retreatants to respond to the following questions:

- What is this game usually called? (*War*)
- What is different about the way I asked you to play the game this time?
- What can we learn from this activity?

Summarize the groups' answers and then continue by offering these comments:

> We need to move away from movies, video games, and other forms of entertainment that glorify violence and find ways to interact more peacefully and feel full of peace in all we do, even in something as simple as playing a card game.
>
> In sports, school, work, and business, we need to foster cooperation rather than competition.

4. Conclude by inviting the retreatants to join in singing the refrain to "We Are Called," or the alternative song the group has been singing throughout the retreat.

If You Want Peace, Work for Justice (1:40 P.M.)

Preparation

- Gather the following supplies:
  - ❑ a TV and VCR or DVD player
  - ❑ the video or DVD titled "In the Footsteps of Jesus: Catholic Social Teaching at Work Today" (United States Conference of Catholic Bishops, Washington, D.C., 2003). If you do not have access to this video, an alternative approach would be to develop a short presentation highlighting Catholic social teachings.
- Set up the TV and VCR in a location where all retreatants can easily view them.

1. Introduce this portion of the retreat in the following way:

> Catholic social teaching begins with the belief that we are all created in the image and likeness of God. Therefore, each person must be treated with respect and dignity. Our Catholic faith demands that we live out the Gospel by ensuring the rights of each person. In this presentation, you will learn more about the basic concepts of Catholic social teaching, or the direction the Church asks us to take in working for the common good of all.
>
> For the next few minutes, we will be watching a video that will help us understand and explore more fully the Church's teachings on justice.

2. Invite the retreatants to jot down each of the Catholic social teachings they hear about in the video as well as any other key points they derive from it. Allow 5 minutes for journal writing after part 1 and part 2 of the video.

Footprints, Fingerprints, and Friendships (2:10 P.M.)

Preparation

- Gather the following supplies:
  - ❏ newsprint
  - ❏ markers
- Write the following questions on newsprint so everyone can see them:
  - ❏ Footprints: What do we leave behind?
  - ❏ Fingerprints: How can we touch people?
  - ❏ Friendships: How can our relationships help us lead a just life?

1. Introduce this activity in the following way:

   During the video, you had a chance to reflect on Catholic social teachings. Now you have an opportunity to look more closely at one teaching. We invite you to explore one teaching by answering these questions, which are listed on the newsprint.

2. When everyone has had ample time for discussion, invite each small group to share its "teaching" and responses to the questions with the large group.

Break (3:00 P.M.)

Passion for Justice Talk 3 (3:20 P.M.)

Preparation

- Ask a team member to prepare a 15-minute talk on justice. To help the person prepare, give him or her a copy of resource 19, "Suggestions for the Passion for Justice Talk," as well as a copy of appendix A, "Helpful Hints for Giving Talks."

1. Introduce the team member giving this talk.

Beatitudes for Living (3:40 P.M.)

Preparation

- Gather the following supplies:
  - ❏ copies of handout 18, "The Beatitudes: Examining Our Conscience," one for each retreatant

1. Distribute a copy of handout 18 to each retreatant. Then introduce this activity in the following way:

   During every retreat, time is set aside for you to be by yourself to have some quiet time.

   We live in such a busy, noisy world (*give examples*) that we often have little time for quiet. Yet, quiet time can help us reflect more on our relationships with ourselves, with others, and with God.

   An examination of conscience is often done in preparation for confessing our sins and receiving the sacrament of Penance and Reconciliation. It is a chance to see how we are doing in our relationships with God and with others. It can also be a way of considering whether we are living our lives justly. This activity uses the Beatitudes of Jesus as a start for reflection.

2. Tell the retreatants that during the next 40 minutes, they may stay inside or go outside, sit under a tree, or go for a walk. Each person must spend the time alone. People should not speak at all until the quiet time is over. During quiet time, they may pray using the handout provided or write in their journals, or both. Ask if they have any questions. Ask them to look at their watches and note the time when quiet time will end. Ask them to meet together at that time so you can review directions, boundaries, and options for free-time activities.

Free Time (4:00 P.M.)

Dinner (5:30 P.M.)

What Is Your Kindness Quotient? (6:30 P.M.)

1. Begin by sharing your own story of how kindness has touched or moved you in some way. Talk about the ways in which small acts of kindness can be quite powerful. Yet kindness, as a quality to strive for, is often overlooked.

2. Invite the small groups to do the following:

- Write a short definition of *kindness.*
- Create a quiz to check retreatants' "kindness quotients."
- Make a list of "random acts of kindness."

You might want to provide the retreatants with this example of a kindness quiz:

- Do you hold the door open for others who follow you?
- Do you really mean it when you say to someone, "How are you doing?"
- Do you offer to clean up after someone else after a meal?
- Do you call or send a card when you learn someone is sick or feeling down?
- When you see someone standing apart from a group, do you go over and say hi?

3. Conclude by encouraging the retreatants to look for opportunities to be kinder in all their relationships. Challenge them to go home and commit "random acts of kindness."

Note: If time permits, invite the small groups to exchange quizzes.

Forming the Justice League (7:00 P.M.)

Preparation

- Gather the following supplies:
  - ❏ newsprint
  - ❏ markers

1. Begin by asking retreatants to call out the names of superheroes from comic strips or movies and the traits that make these heroes special. List the names and traits on newsprint.

2. Tell the retreatants that each small group will create a superhero to fight injustice in a nonviolent way. Group members need to work together on this project. To do this, they will need to answer the following questions:

- What is the name of your superhero?
- What issue does he or she champion?
- What type of costume does he or she wear?
- What are his or her superpowers?
- How does he or she fight for change in a nonviolent way?

You may want to list these questions on newsprint so the groups can refer to them.

3. Provide each small group with markers and one or two sheets of newsprint. Give the groups about 40 minutes to work together on this project.

4. Invite each group to come forward and share a little about the superhero they have created. Close by reminding retreatants of the everyday heroes that work for justice and how each of us can do our part to make a difference. We can choose heroes who champion justice and raise them up, and we can each work in our own way to make a small difference, with our words and actions, every day.

Break (8:00 P.M.)

Passion for Justice Talk 4 (8:30 P.M.)

Preparation

- Ask a team member to prepare a 15-minute talk on justice. To help the person prepare, give him or her a copy of resource 19, "Suggestions for the Passion for Justice Talk," as well as a copy of appendix A, "Helpful Hints for Giving Talks."

1. Introduce the team member giving this talk.

2. After the talk, allow 5 minutes for reflection and journal writing.

TV Shows and Justice (8:50 P.M.)

Preparation

- Gather the following supplies:
  - ❑ three TVs
  - ❑ three VCRs or DVD players
  - ❑ videotapes or DVDs of one episode from three different TV shows (Choose episodes from three different shows that feature three different social justice themes. Make sure the shows are acceptable for family viewing.)
- Set up the TVs and VCRs or DVD players in three different locations.

Note: If you do not have access to three TVs, you can have the retreatants view one show instead.

1. Divide the retreatants into three groups. Tell them that each group will be watching an episode of a different television show. Allow them to move to their designated spaces and get settled. Then watch the shows.

2. Allow 20 minutes for discussion. Ask the groups to reflect on what they have learned from the episode. Ask them to identify other TV shows, movies, or videos that have highlighted social justice themes. Ask each group to choose one person to take notes and another to serve as a spokesperson.

3. If time permits, spokespeople from each of the three groups should
   - give a synopsis of the show they watched
   - give highlights of their discussion
   - give other examples of TV shows or movies with social justice themes

4. Urge the retreatants to be discriminating when they choose to watch TV shows or movies, play video games, or listen to music. Encourage them to build awareness of social justice issues by avoiding shows, movies, games, or music with negative messages.

Snack and Free Time (9:30 P.M.)

A Season for Nonviolence (10:30 P.M.)

Preparation

- Gather the following supplies:
  - ❑ several votive candles
  - ❑ taper candles, one for each retreatant
  - ❑ a CD player
  - ❑ a CD with a contemporary song about peace
  - ❑ a CD with a liturgical hymn for peace
  - ❑ ten copies of resource 23, "Prayer Vigil"

- Recruit eight team members to assist with the vigil. Provide each with a copy of resource 23 and assign parts accordingly.
- Choose one contemporary song about peace and one liturgical hymn for peace to use during the prayer service. Both can be played for reflection or one can be sung by the group together.
- Place the candles on a nearby table.
- Be sure that the songbooks or hymnals have been moved to the prayer space.

1. Invite the retreatants to join you in the prayer space. Distribute the hymnals or songbooks to everyone. Allow a few moments for everyone to get settled. Then proceed with the prayer vigil as noted on resource 23.

Note: Be sure to return the songbooks to the small-group tables.

Lights Out (12:00 A.M.)

Detailed Description of Activities for Sunday

Rising (7:45 A.M.)

Breakfast (8:30 A.M.)

If We Are the Body, Why Aren't Our Hands Reaching? (9:00 A.M.)

Preparation

- Gather the following supplies:
  - ❑ a CD with the song "If We Are the Body," by Casting Crowns. Or choose a song that reflects the theme of the Body of Christ.
  - ❑ a CD player
  - ❑ three copies of resource 24, "We Are the Body"
- Recruit two team members to assist with this prayer. Provide each with a copy of resource 24 and a copy of *The Catholic Youth Bible* or another Bible.

1. Invite all the retreatants to join you in the prayer space. Allow a few moments for everyone to get settled. Proceed with the prayer service as noted on resource 24.

Passion for Justice Talk 5 (9:30 A.M.)

Preparation

- Ask a team member to prepare a 15-minute talk on justice. To help the person prepare, give him or her a copy of resource 19, "Suggestions for the Passion for Justice Talk," as well as a copy of appendix A, "Helpful Hints for Giving Talks."

1. Introduce the team member giving this talk.

2. After the talk, allow 5 minutes for reflection and journal writing.

The Baby That Floated Downstream (9:50 A.M.)

Preparation

- Read over the story below (steps 1–5) and familiarize yourself with it so you can tell the story in your own words rather than just read it.

1. Tell the following story:

   Imagine that you live in utopia. Everybody and everything is perfect. Everyone gets along, and there is always someone available to help you if you need it. There is plenty of food and water. You have a loving family and plenty of friends. You have everything you need to be content.

   One day you are out by the river for a picnic with friends, enjoying a beautiful day playing and splashing in the water. Suddenly you see a baby floating down the river in a basket. The baby is very sick and bruised. The baby is hungry and near death.

   What would you do if this happened to you? (*Pause for a moment and let the retreatants ponder this question.*)

2. Continue:

   You take the baby out of the water and carry him home. You feed him and take him to the doctor for medicine. You care for his wounds and nurse him back to health. You buy clothes and a crib and give him a lot of love and attention. He begins to thrive. You adopt him and make him part of your family.

   A month later, you and your baby and your friends are again enjoying a day by the river. This time, you see two babies in baskets floating down the river. The babies are very sick and bruised. They are hungry and near death.

   What would you and your friends do now? (*Pause for a moment and let the retreatants ponder this question.*)

3. Continue:

   So you take the babies out of the water. Your friends take the two girls home. They feed the babies and take them to the doctor for medicine. They care for their wounds and nurse them back to health. They buy clothes and a crib and give the girls a lot of love and attention, and they begin to thrive. They adopt the girls and make them part of their families.

   Three months later, you and your baby and your friends and their babies are again enjoying a day by the river, when all of a sudden the river is completely full of babies floating in baskets. The babies are very sick and bruised. They are hungry and near death.

   What would you and your friends do now? (*Pause for a moment and let the retreatants ponder this question.*)

4. At least one retreatant will realize that it is time to take a trip upstream and find out what is going on. Summarize peoples' responses, and continue with these comments:

> We cannot just keep taking care of the babies and others in need that float downstream into our lives. We cannot just keep giving out charity individually. We need to advocate for social change.
>
> We need to go upstream and find out why so many babies are sick and dying and why their families are abandoning them to the river. We need to find the causes of poverty and other injustices and work to find some solutions, one step at a time, one day at a time. This can mean working within our local communities, but it can also mean that we must write letters and seek to change local or state laws that affect social justice issues.

5. Invite the retreatants to open their songbooks and join in singing the refrain to "We Are Called" or the song you have been singing throughout the retreat.

Action Keys (10:00 A.M.)

Preparation

- Several weeks before the retreat, identify one possible way to take some action on a social justice issue or concern. This should be an action that the retreatants can begin during the retreat (like a letter-writing campaign). You may want to consult with the parish peace and justice minister or committee or dovetail your activity with a project already planned for the parish. Make sure that the project you select includes both a direct service and a social action component.

1. Conduct the activity you have chosen.

Break (10:45 A.M.)

Finding Nemo, Swimming Down (11:00 A.M.)

Preparation

- Gather the following supplies:
  - ❑ a TV
  - ❑ a VCR or DVD player
  - ❑ a copy of the movie *Finding Nemo* (Walt Disney Productions, 2003, rated G, 100 minutes)
- Familiarize yourself with *Finding Nemo*. If you have never seen the movie, you will want to watch it in its entirety or at least familiarize yourself with the segment discussed below.
- Cue up the following segment from the movie: Dory and a large school of fish become trapped in a fishing net. (It is approximately 85 minutes into the movie and is designated "Scene 28: Fishing Net" in the DVD scene selection list.)

1. Provide the retreatants with an overview of the movie. Then show the video clip.

2. When the clip is over, ask the retreatants the following questions:

- What would have happened to the fish if they had been hauled onto the ship?
- How did the fish break free from the net?
- Who gave them the idea to swim down together and break the net?
- What happened to Nemo when he joined the other fish in their struggle to break free?

Invite responses to these questions from several people.

3. Summarize the responses and continue with these comments:

> We will swim in many different directions and go nowhere unless we find a way to work together. Amazing change is possible if we stand up together for what is right. We need courageous leaders with good ideas to organize people for political and economic solutions to problems. Working for change involves a risk. It may take a while before we see any results. However, the effort and the time spent are worth it.

4. Conclude by inviting the retreatants to open their songbooks and join in singing the refrain to "We Are Called," or the song you have been singing throughout the retreat.

Be the Change You Want to See in the World (11:10 A.M.)

Preparation

- Gather the following supplies:
  - ❏ copies of handout 19, "Oscar Romero's Prayer," one for each retreatant
- Ask a team member to weave together the highlights of the retreat into a 15-minute talk. To help the person prepare, give him or her a copy of resource 25, "Suggestions for the Be the Change Talk," as well as a copy of appendix A, "Helpful Hints for Giving Talks."

1. Introduce the team member giving this talk.

2. After the talk, give each person a copy of handout 19, and allow 5 minutes for quiet reflection and journal writing.

Weaving Justice (11:30 A.M.)

Preparation

- Gather the following supplies:
  - ❏ 2-by-18-inch strips of multicolored construction paper, three strips for each person
  - ❏ staplers and staples
  - ❏ markers

1. Give each person three different colored strips of construction paper and a marker. Give each small group a stapler. Invite everyone to do the following:

On the first strip of paper, write your first and last names to symbolize your commitment to work for peace and justice in your own way.

On the second strip of paper, write one peace and justice issue that has touched your heart this weekend.

On the third strip of paper, write a Scripture passage or prayer that has lifted your spirits this weekend.

2. Invite the small groups to share their responses. Invite the groups to weave the strips of construction paper into a colorful tapestry, leaving small gaps between strips, and staple the strips securely together so the tapestry can be displayed.

3. Challenge the retreatants to continue weaving Micah 6:8 and the Gospel message into their lives so they can leave as a legacy a tapestry of hope.

4. Display the tapestry prominently as part of the environment for celebrating Mass together.

Lunch (12:15 P.M.)

Preparation for Liturgy (1:00 P.M.)

Closing Liturgy (1:45 P.M.)

Alternative Ideas for This Retreat

Here are some activity ideas that can be used for a longer version of this retreat or as alternative activities:

- Divide the large group into four small groups. Assign each small group one of the Gospels. Instead of selecting Scripture passages ahead of time for the groups to study, ask each group to find at least ten passages in which Jesus gives us an example of how we are to live justly. Each group can then choose one passage for further study and reflection.
- Instead of finding justice themes in TV shows, ask the retreatants to look for themes in popular music.
- Ask the retreatants to make a connection between the works of mercy and specific Scripture passages. A connection may also be made between the works of mercy and the Catholic social teaching themes.
- Handout 15, "The Two Feet of Christian Service," and the accompanying activity in retreat 4 could be used as part of retreat 5.

Resource 17

Suggestions for the Welcome and Opening Talk

This talk welcomes the retreatants and introduces the retreat team. It prepares the retreatants for what they will experience during the weekend. You have about 10 minutes for this presentation. The following ideas and thought starters may be helpful.

Welcome

- Greet the retreatants and let them know how happy the team is that they have decided to come. Then introduce the team members. Share your own retreat experiences by talking about some of the following topics:
  - Your reasons for being part of the retreat team
  - Your fears about your first retreat (e.g., how you reacted to the other people, the talks, the activities)
  - How your feelings changed throughout your first retreat experience and how the retreat changed your relationship with God
- Emphasize that everyone has something valuable to share and that everyone will have an important part in making the retreat weekend a success.

Goals of Retreat

Provide an overview of the goals for the weekend:

- To learn more about oneself
- To learn more about one another
- To grow closer to God

Introduction to Journal Writing

- Explain that the retreatants will spend some time during the weekend writing in a journal. A journal helps people get in touch with their feelings. Ask the following question: Why is writing about something often easier than talking about it?
- Discuss the way the retreatants will use their journals to write their reactions to talks and activities. Ask everyone to bring their journals to every activity during the weekend and to write in them often. Stress the importance of respecting the privacy of each person's journal.

Resource 18

Suggestions for the Micah 6:8 Talk

This talk is meant to introduce the theme of the retreat and to help people begin to reflect on this powerful Scripture passage. You have about 20 minutes for this presentation. The following provides ideas and thought starters.

Seeing with New Eyes

- At this retreat, we invite you to look at yourself, others, and the world through different eyes, through the eyes of Jesus.
- Some examples of seeing with new eyes are . . .
- How we look at the world affects how we approach peace and justice issues. Do you look at the world as half empty or half full?
- Share Micah 6:8. Tell retreatants that Micah was a prophet from a small town who was sent to a big town. He communicated God's promises but also communicated God's warnings.

Do Justice

- We are called not just to read about justice, not just to think about justice, not just to talk about justice, but to do justice.
- We are going to talk about a lot of different issues, most only briefly. This is Social Justice 101; it will not be all you need to know. This is a taste, to make you more aware, to spur you to action. We cannot cover all the issues in one weekend.
- Here is our challenge: How can we weave justice through our lives?

Love Kindness

- What do you think about when people say you are a kind person? It is not always considered a compliment. It is often considered better to be assertive or tough.
- We are called to love kindness, to keep it close to our hearts, to keep others close to our hearts.
- Give some examples of ways you have experienced the kindness of others.
- Give some examples of how you have learned to express kindness in your life.
- Here is our challenge: How can we weave kindness through our lives?

Walk Humbly with Your God

- Humility comes from looking at the cross and saying: "He died for me?"
- Just imagine how different our lives would be if we recognized God walking next to us as we go through our day. God is in this place and right here with us now. God created me and formed me. God knew me before I was born. All I do, I do through the grace of God. I trust God. I put my life in God's hands.

Handout 16

World Awareness Quiz

1. How many people in the world live on less than one dollar per day?

   A. 500 million B. 1.2 billion C. 875 million

2. How many people in the United States live in a state of poverty, hunger, and hardship?

   A. 47 million B. 36 million C. 8.5 million

3. How many people in the world suffer from hunger, unable to afford enough food, the most basic necessity of life?

   A. 852 million B. 427 million C. 1 billion

4. The amount of money earned by the wealthiest one percent of the world's population equals the amount of money earned by the poorest ______ of the world's population.

   A. 9% B. 32% C. 57%

5. How many people in the world are infected with HIV/AIDS?

   A. 42 million B. 27 million C. 59 million

6. How many people in the world do not have access to clean water?

   A. 68 million B. 496 million C. 1.1 billion

7. In the United States, the average water usage per person per day is ______.

   A. 56 gallons B. 100 gallons C. 235 gallons

(This quiz is taken from Catholic Relief Services [CRS], *2006 Educator's Guide* [Baltimore: MD: CRS, 2005], page 39. Copyright © 2005 by CRS. Used with permission.)

Handout 17

World Awareness Quiz Answers

1. (B) 1.2 billion people in the developing world earn less than one dollar per day and, therefore, live below the international poverty line. (Bread for the World Web site)

2. (B) 36 million people in the United States, or about 12.5% of the population, live in poverty. (Poverty USA Web site)

3. (A) 852 million people in the world suffer from hunger. (Bread for the World Web site)

4. (C) The amount of money that the wealthiest one percent of the world's population makes equals the amount of money that the poorest 57% of the world's population makes. (United Nations Web site)

5. (A) 42 million people worldwide are infected with HIV/AIDS. (Catholic Relief Services Web site)

6. (C) 1.1 billion people lack access to clean water; nearly 2 billion people lack safe sanitation. More than 3 million people still die every year from avoidable water-related diseases. (World Bank Web site)

7. (B) In the United States, the average person uses about 100 gallons of water a day. (National Geographic Web site)

(These answers are taken from Catholic Relief Services [CRS], *2006 Educator's Guide* [Baltimore: MD: CRS, 2005], page 40. Copyright © 2005 by CRS. Used with permission.)

Resource 19

Suggestions for the Passion for Justice Talk

Choose a Topic

This talk is meant to introduce various justice themes and issues. Choose a topic that you have encountered through service, that you want to learn more about, or that you feel passionately about. Here are some possibilities: poverty, racism, violence, war, abortion, abuse, hunger, crime, neglect, sexism, globalization, death penalty, homophobia, illiteracy, euthanasia, greed, pollution. You have about 20 minutes for this presentation. The following ideas and thought starters may be helpful.

Share What You Have Learned About This Issue

- What are the basic facts and information about the issue?
- Who is most affected?
- Why should this be an issue that the retreatants should care about?

Share Some Examples of the Impact of This Issue

- Tell a story or two about someone you know (or have heard about) that has been affected by this issue.
- Talk about how this issue has personally affected you (directly or indirectly).

Make a Scripture Connection

- Search the Scriptures for passages that relate to your topic.

Talk About How You Feel About This Issue

- How has this issue affected your own thinking or belief system?
- In what ways have you gotten involved with this issue?
- What else would you like to be doing to address this issue?

How Can We Become More Aware of This Issue?

- How can others learn more about the issue?
- Offer some ideas for involvement.
- What are some action steps we can take to start making a difference?

Resource 20

Standing with Those Who Have Made a Difference

Prayer Leader: Today we gather in prayer to thank God for the gift of Jesus and his inspiration to us to take a stand and make a difference in the world. We pray for courage to follow his example in our everyday lives. We now join in prayer with those who have gone before and stood up for what is right and good.

(Invite each reader to stand to read his or her role and remain standing as the prayer continues.)

Voices of the Just

Voice 1: My name is Mother Teresa. I worked with the poorest of the poor in India, the outcasts, the people no one cared about and would never touch. Like Saint Teresa of Ávila, I believe that Jesus has no hands but our own. Won't you reach out to the poor with me?

Voice 2: My name is Dorothy Day. I founded Catholic Worker House, which provided a haven for the poor and needy. I championed the right of workers to receive a just wage. I believe that social change can be achieved only through nonviolence. Won't you work for change with me?

Voice 3: My name is Archbishop Romero. I led the Church in El Salvador and worked tirelessly to bring social justice to my country. I tried to end government violence against the poor. My stands made me very unpopular. I was assassinated while saying Mass in March of 1980. Won't you stand against violence with me?

Voice 4: My name is Maximillian Kolbe. I am a Polish Franciscan priest who was imprisoned during World War II in Auschwitz, a Nazi concentration camp. I volunteered to take the place of a young father condemned to starve to death. Won't you place the needs of others before yourself?

Voice 5: My name is Sr. Thea Bowman. I am a singer, an evangelist, and a member of the Franciscan Sisters of Perpetual Adoration. I am a champion of African American culture. I didn't let cancer stop me from speaking and singing out about what is right. Won't you offer hope and courage to others?

Voice 6: My name is Cardinal Bernardin. I led the Archdiocese of Chicago and chaired the U.S. Bishops' committee that drafted a pastoral letter on war and peace. I was a constant defender of the sanctity and dignity of human life from conception to death. Won't you stand up for the right to life with me?

Voice 7: I am the nameless, faceless person who suffers daily at the hands of others. I am the person who needs your love and compassion. I am the sick, the imprisoned, and the babies who will never be born. I am the old, the young, and the poorest of the poor. I am the people who yearn for peace and still hope for justice. I am Jesus. Won't you stand with me?

Concluding Prayer

Prayer Leader: Let us pray.
Loving God, you created us as a gift for one another.
Give us eyes to see all who are in need or are being treated unjustly in our world.
Give us ears to hear people who call for help.
Give us willing arms to reach out and touch others who need to feel your presence.
Most of all, give us courage to stand up for others and for what we believe.
We ask this through Christ our Lord.
Amen.

(This prayer service is adapted from Maryann Hakowski, *22 Ready-Made Prayer Services with 100 Extra Prayer Ideas* [Winona, MN: Saint Mary's Press, 2006], pages 33–34.

Resource 21

Walking in Another's Shoes

Prayer Leader: The Gospel calls us to be hope for those who are poor. Let us listen to the voices of teens, in our country and throughout the world, that desperately need hope. Let us add our prayers to their voices. Our response is, "We will love you and pray for you." **All respond.**

Voice 1: My name is Josef. I have lived my whole life in a country torn apart by war. I am always afraid. I can only dream of what it must be like to live in peace. Please pray for me, my sisters and brothers. **All respond.**

Voice 2: My name is Miguel. A hurricane came through and destroyed our island. There is nothing left where my home once stood. I can't even find some of my friends. Please pray for me, my brothers and sisters. **All respond.**

Voice 3: My name is Sanche. Our land has been without rain for a long time. Nothing grows here any more. We sometimes go for days without anything to eat. And many of us are dying. Please pray for us, my sisters and brothers. **All respond.**

Voice 4: My name is Anna, but you will never meet me. I will never get to live a life like yours and see the pain and joy of being a teenager. My mother decided to have an abortion. Please pray for me, my brothers and sisters. **All respond.**

Voice 5: My name is Matthew. It all started at a party where everyone was trying cocaine. I never thought I could get addicted. Now all I think about every minute is getting more coke. Please pray for me, my sisters and brothers. **All respond.**

Voice 6: My name is Andrew. My parents are going through a divorce. All they do is fight and blame me for everything. I feel like I am torn apart. I want it all to end. Please pray for me, my brothers and sisters. **All respond.**

Voice 7: My name is Kristin. I ran away from home when I was twelve, and I have lived on the street for two years. Most of the time I am hungry, cold, and scared. I wonder if I can ever go home again. Please pray for me, my sisters and brothers. **All respond.**

Voice 8: My name is Jean. I am really frightened about growing up when I see all the awful things that are going on in the world. It is almost as if people have forgotten all about God. Please pray for all of us, my brothers and sisters. **All respond.**

Prayer Leader: Sisters and brothers, we offer these prayers to our Lord, Jesus, who not only calls us to hope but also to help build a just and peaceful world. We offer these prayers of hope in the name of the risen Lord. Amen.

(Adapted from Maryann Hakowski, *22 Ready-Made Prayer Services with 100 Extra Prayer Ideas* [Winona, MN: Saint Mary's Press, 2006], pages 27–29.

Resource 22

Suggestions for the Jesus and Justice Talk

This talk explores how Jesus lived a just life through his words and actions. You have about 15 minutes for the presentation. The following ideas and thought starters may be helpful.

What Does the Lord Require of You but to . . . Do Justice

- Jesus showed special care for those who the rest of society had scorned or forgotten. He touched lepers, cured those with disabilities, worried about widows. He talked to prostitutes and ate at the houses of tax collectors.
- Jesus chose to live a simple lifestyle. He showed great respect for all of God's creation. Rather than exploit elements of nature, he used them as examples for teaching about the Reign of God.
- Jesus introduced a whole new way of treating others.
- He was not afraid of challenging the norms of society. He refused to answer violence with violence, even when he faced his own death.
- He even forgave those who crucified him, from the cross where he was hanging.
- Jesus always put people before things.
- In the Beatitudes (see Matthew 5:1–12), Jesus gives us a wonderful guide for setting our priorities. How can we thirst for what is right? How are we challenged to be peacemakers?
- Jesus recognized and celebrated the worth of each person.
- He saw the great dignity in each person.
- How does Jesus inspire you to live? Give some examples from your experiences.
- How does Jesus challenge us to build God's Reign here on earth?
- Challenge the retreatants to follow the example of Jesus in their everyday lives.

Handout 18

The Beatitudes: Examining Our Conscience

This examination of conscience is based on the Beatitudes found in Matthew 5:1–13. Prayerfully reflect on the questions and then write about your overall experience in your journal.

"Blessed are the poor in spirit, for theirs is the kingdom of heaven."

- Do I fear being poor, in spirit or otherwise, and prefer to be rich in money or power?
- Do I contribute my time, talent, and money to the poor of the world?
- Do I look for the causes of poverty and seek solutions to changing unjust systems?

"Blessed are those who mourn, for they shall be comforted."

- Do I grieve over loneliness, despair, guilt, and rejection in the lives of others?
- Am I willing to admit my own worries and fears and need for comfort?
- Am I doing anything to dry the tears of those who are in mourning over war, poverty, hunger, injustice?

"Blessed are the meek, for they shall inherit the earth."

- Do I see any value in meekness or nonviolence?
- Do I cringe at the thought of being called meek?
- Do I favor cooperation over competition?

"Blessed are those who hunger and thirst for righteousness, for they will be satisfied."

- Have I kept silent when I should have spoken out against prejudice, injustice, and violence?
- Am I aware of current events and issues of injustice?
- Do I honestly try to improve the quality of life around me?

"Blessed are the merciful, for they shall obtain mercy."

- Do I operate on a double standard of expecting mercy but not wanting to grant it?
- Are there people in my life who are suffering because of my unforgiving attitude?
- Am I a person of mercy, tenderness, and compassion?

"Blessed are the pure in heart, for they shall see God."

- Am I open and honest about who I am and what I do?
- Am I trusting and trustful?
- Have I failed to take time for prayer, quiet, and reflection?

"Blessed are the peacemakers, for they shall be called children of God."

- Do I think apologizing is a sign of weakness?
- Do I accept violence in films, television, and sports?
- Do I build bridges or walls in family arguments?

"Blessed are those who are persecuted for righteousness' sake, for theirs is the kingdom of heaven. Blessed are you when people revile you and persecute you and utter all kinds of evil against you falsely on my account."

- Am I embarrassed to stand up for what is right?
- Have I called myself a Christian without living the way I should?
- Do I support those who openly defend justice for others?

"Rejoice and be glad, for your reward in heaven is great."

- Do I believe that the cross of Jesus Christ can conquer injustice with peace and love?
- Am I a source of hope for others?
- Does my faith in God bring me joy?

(Adapted from "Examination of Conscience," by Doris Donnelly, in *The Fire of Peace*, edited by Mary Lou Kownacki [Erie, PA: Pax Christi USA, 1992], pages 224–228. Copyright © 1992 by Pax Christi USA. Used with permission.)

Resource 23

Prayer Vigil

Leader 1: We gather in the name of peace. Let there be peace on earth.

Leader 2: We gather, each from our own tradition,

To pray for peace and an end to all violence;
Among cultures and between nations;
Among faiths and between denominations;
Among families and between persons.

We pray for an end to all acts of violence and hatred.

Reader 1: Peace can only last where human rights are respected, where the people are fed, and where individuals and nations are free. (The Dalai Lama)

(Light first candle.)

Leader 1: Where do we begin? There are so many who lack basic human rights. There are so many who are hungry. And so many who do not know what it is like to be free. Let us reflect on these words from the Dalai Lama and pray for peace throughout the world.

(Pause for a few moments of silence.)

Reader 2: Nothing I can do or say will change the structure of the universe. But maybe, by raising my voice, I can help the greatest of all causes: goodwill among [all] and peace on earth. (Albert Einstein)

(Light second candle.)

Leader 1: Let us reflect on these words from Albert Einstein. How can you raise your voice for peace?

(Pause for a few moments of silence.)

Reader 3: You cannot shake hands with a clenched fist. (Indira Gandhi)

(Light third candle.)

Leader 1: When we gather for Mass, the presider says, "Peace be with you." And we respond, "And also with you." And then we offer one another a sign of peace. Let us reflect on these words from Indira Gandhi and pray to become a living sign of God's peace, not just at Mass for a minute or two but every day in every way.

(Pause for a few moments of silence.)

Reader 4: If you want peace, work for justice. (Pope Paul VI)

(Light fourth candle.)

Leader 1: Let us reflect on this powerful message from Pope Paul VI. Pray it silently over and over, like a mantra, and allow the prayer to become part of you.

(Pause for a few moments of silence.)

(Play the first song for peace.)

Scripture Reader 1: *(Proclaim Ecclesiastes 3:1–8.)*

(Light fifth candle.)

Leader 2: Reflect on some of the fighting in the world right now, particularly places in the world that see a lot of conflict. Now is a time for prayer, prayer for peace in the world.

(Pause for a few moments of silence.)

Scripture Reader 2: (*Proclaim Isaiah 9:6.*)

(Light sixth candle.)

Leader 2: There are many different names for God and many different ways to relate to God. Reflect on God as prince of peace, as peacemaker. How can you bring the peace of the prince of peace into your everyday life?

(Pause for a few moments of silence.)

Scripture Reader 3: (*Proclaim Matthew 5:9.*)

(Light seventh candle.)

Leader 2: Peacemakers do not sit around waiting for peace to happen. They make peace at every opportunity. Reflect on the relationships between members of your family. How can you be a peacemaker in your family?

(Pause for a few moments of silence.)

Scripture Reader 4: (*Proclaim John 14:19–21.*)

(Light eighth candle.)

Leader 2: The peace of Christ is not just to savor, not just to keep to ourselves. Jesus gives us the gift of peace, then sends us forth to proclaim the Gospel. Where does God need to send you right now with his peace? to school? to work? to church?

(Pause for a few moments of silence.)

(Invite everyone to join in singing the song you have selected.)

(While singing, invite the retreatants, one at a time, to light their candles from one of the votive candles already lit in the center of the prayer space.)

Leader 1: Please extend your hands over one another and repeat after me:
Dear Lord, prince of peace,
Bless your servants gathered here.
May we live your call to be peacemakers
In our world, in our nation
In our schools, in our work
And in our families.
Amen.

(The quotations on this resource are taken from the Waging Peace Web site.)

Resource 24

We Are the Body

Reader 1: If we are the body, why aren't our hands reaching?

First Reading: James 2:1–9

Leader: If we are the body, why aren't our hands reaching?

Song Reflection: "If We Are the Body," by Casting Crowns, or the alternative song you have chosen

Second Reading: John 5:19–21

Reader 1: If we are the body, why aren't our hands reaching?

Leader: We ask you to join in with any special intentions at this time.
Our response will be: Lord hear our prayer.

(Invite the retreatants to voice their petitions at this time.)

Reader 1: If we are the body, why aren't our hands reaching?

Leader: Kind God, we thank you for all the blessings you have so richly given us. So we come to you with heavy hearts at this time. There's a lack of justice in the world. People are more concerned with padding their own pockets than with judging others fairly. We see evidence of this in the legal system that governs us, and, yes, even in the Church. God, we ask that you guide us in the path that we should take. Show us that your way is a better way, and if we follow it we will be much better off. This I pray in the name of your Son, Jesus Christ. Amen.

Handout 19

Oscar Romero's Prayer

It helps, now and then, to step back and take the long view.
The kingdom is not only beyond our efforts, it is even beyond our vision.
We accomplish in our lifetime only a tiny fraction of the magnificent enterprise that is God's work. Nothing we do is complete, which is a way of saying that the kingdom always lies beyond us.
No statement says all that could be said.
No prayer fully expresses our faith.
No confession brings perfection.
No pastoral visit brings wholeness.
No program accomplishes the Church's mission.
No set of goals and objectives includes everything.
This is what we are about.
We plant the seeds that one day will grow.
We water seeds already planted, knowing that they hold future promise.
We lay foundations that will need further development.
We provide yeast that produces far beyond our capabilities.

We cannot do everything, and there is a sense of liberation in realizing that.
This enables us to do something and to do it very well.
It may be incomplete, but it is a beginning, a step along the way, an opportunity for the Lord's grace to enter and do the rest.
We may never see the end results, but that is the difference between the master builder and the worker.
We are workers, not master builders; ministers, not messiahs.
We are prophets of a future not our own.
Amen.

(This prayer is taken from the Xaverian Missionaries Web site.)

Resource 25

Suggestions for the Be the Change Talk

This talk highlights the key thoughts and experiences of the retreat. It challenges the retreatants to leave the retreat and put what they have learned into action.

A Good Listener, a Good Observer

Yours is the only talk that cannot be prepared before the retreat. You need to be a good listener. Take lots of notes. Capture the key points of the other talks. Jot down the insights learned to live this Scripture in the last few days.

- How have you learned to live this Scripture in the last few days?

Where Do We Go from Here?

The most important part of this talk is the challenge: "Be the change you want to see in the world."

A Powerful Prayer

Close with the prayer from Oscar Romero. Read or proclaim it with the retreatants and ask them to quietly reflect on it in their journals.

Appendix A

Helpful Hints for Giving Talks

- Speak slowly and thoughtfully.
- Try to maintain eye contact with your audience.
- Share examples and stories from your own life.
- Share your feelings; be open and honest.
- Use a Scripture passage, a song, or a poem to help make a point.
- Explore the use of symbols (e.g., give out a nail when you invite retreatants to join you on the way to the cross).
- Use humor if you are comfortable with it.
- Stay within your time frame. Talks that are too short fail to challenge listeners, and talks that are too long fail to keep the attention of listeners.
- Stay focused on your topic. You may not need to elucidate all the points, but you need to discuss fully the main theme of your talk.
- Practice giving your talk to someone before the retreat and ask for feedback.
- End with a question or a challenge for the retreatants; leave your audience with something on which to reflect.
- Most important, be yourself.

Appendix B

Guidelines for Retreat Team Leaders

Throughout the Retreat

1. Familiarize yourself with the retreat so you will be better able to clarify directions given by the retreat coordinator and other team members.
2. Participate in all activities and discussions during the retreat.
3. Help give out supplies and get the retreat space ready for activities.
4. Follow all retreat ground rules and assist in enforcing these rules.
5. Set a good example by respecting and listening to the speakers.
6. Help all the retreatants feel welcome and comfortable.
7. Lead, encourage, affirm, support, and befriend the retreatants.

In Small Groups

1. Help each person in your small group to get to know the others better.
2. If you have trouble getting things started, try this: Begin with the person who has the next birthday, has the most letters in her or his last name, is wearing green, has a shirt with a sports logo on it, has the most siblings, and so on.
3. Be aware of the shy people (who need more encouragement) and the rowdy ones (who need some calming down). It also helps to know if a young person is struggling with a loss or going through personal problems.
4. Keep to the given activity's topic and guide the discussion.
5. Contribute to, but do not dominate, the discussion.
6. Avoid "yes" or "no" questions that tend to shut down conversation. Instead, ask open-ended questions:
   - How do you feel?
   - What is your reaction to the talk?
   - What would you write for that question?
   - What do you think?
7. Do a lot of listening.
8. Make sure each person has a chance to contribute to the discussion; stress that each person's contribution is valuable.
9. Thank each person for her or his contribution.
10. Share your own responses, experiences, and ideas honestly and openly.
11. Do not be afraid to share your faith.

Appendix C

Index of Activities

Acknowledgments

The scriptural quotations contained herein are from the New Revised Standard Version of the Bible, Catholic Edition. Copyright © 1993 and 1989 by the Division of Christian Education of the National Council of the Churches of Christ in the United States of America. All rights reserved.

The prayers, devotions, beliefs, and practices contained herein have been verified against authoritative sources.

The song lyrics on page 5 are from the sheet music of "Farewell Blessing" (Portland, OR: OCP Publications). Text copyright © 1991 by Gary Hardin and James Hansen, 5536 NE Hassalo, Portland, OR 97213. All rights reserved. Used with permission. Published by OCP Publications.

The material on pages 26, 88, 90, 92, and 95–96 that is labeled *The Catholic Faith Handbook for Youth* or *CFH* is from *The Catholic Faith Handbook for Youth*, by Brian Singer-Towns et al. (Winona, MN: Saint Mary's Press, 2004), pages 409, 138–139, 140–141, 139–140, and 307 and 385, respectively. Copyright © 2004 by Saint Mary's Press. All rights reserved.

The steps for *lectio divina* on handout 1 are taken from the workshop "Bringing Youth and the Bible Together." Copyright © 2000 by Saint Mary's Press.

The material for the activity on page 37 and on handout 3 is adapted from *Community Building Ideas for Ministry with Young Teens*, by Marilyn Kielbasa (Winona, MN: Saint Mary's Press, 2001), pages 53–54 and 54–55. Copyright © 2001 by Saint Mary's Press. All rights reserved.

The prayer on page 38 is from *Dreams Alive: Prayers by Teenagers*, edited by Carl Koch (Winona, MN: Saint Mary's Press, 1991), page 56. Copyright © 1991 by Saint Mary's Press. All rights reserved.

The "American Indian Prayer" on handout 7 is from *A Book of Prayers* (Dubuque, IA: Harcourt Religion Publishers, 1990), page 28. Copyright © 1990 by Harcourt Religion Publishers. Used with permission.

The material in "Prayer to Cast Out Demons" on page 61 and resource 6, and the material on resource 16, resource 20, and resource 21 is adapted from *22 Ready-Made Prayer Services with 100 Extra Prayer Ideas*, by Maryann Hakowski (Winona, MN: Saint Mary's Press, 2006), pages 106–107, 45–46, 33–34, and 27–29, respectively. Copyright © 2006 by Saint Mary's Press. All rights reserved.

The "Fishbowl" activity on page 62 and resource 7 is adapted from *Growing with Jesus: Sixteen Half-Day, Full-Day, and Overnite Retreats That Help Children Celebrate and Share the Light of Christ*, by Maryann Hakowski (Notre Dame, IN: Ave Maria Press, 1993), pages 147–148. Copyright © 1993 by Ave Maria Press.

The "Islands of Safety" activity on page 67 is drawn from *Lights for the World: Training Youth Leaders for Peer Ministry*, by Lisa-Marie Calderone-Stewart (Winona, MN: Saint Mary's Press, 1995), pages 62–63. Copyright © 1995 by Saint Mary's Press. All rights reserved.

The "Name That Sacrament" activity on pages 101–102 is from *Vine and Branches Volume 1: Resources for Youth Retreats*, by Maryann Hakowski (Winona, MN: Saint Mary's Press, 1992), pages 40–41. Copyright © 1992 by Saint Mary's Press. All rights reserved.

The lyrics on pages 102–103 and the material on resource 13 are from the *Sacramentary*, English translation prepared by the International Commission on English in the Liturgy (ICEL) (New York: Catholic Book Publishing Company, 1985), pages 173 and 204–205. Excerpts from *The Rite of Holy Week*, © 1970 by the ICEL. All rights reserved. Illustrations and arrangement copyright © 1985–1974 by the Catholic Book Publishing Company, New York. Used with permission.

The "Witness Wear" activity on page 105 is from *Sharing the Sunday Scriptures with Youth, Cycle A: Lectionary-Based Resources for Youth Ministry*, by Maryann Hakowski (Winona, MN: Saint Mary's Press, 1998), page 130. Copyright © 1998 by Saint Mary's Press. All rights reserved.

The material on handout 14 is from *Stations for Teens: Meditations on the Death and Resurrection of Jesus*, by Gary Egeberg (Winona, MN: Saint Mary's Press, 1999), page 13. Copyright © 1999 by Saint Mary's Press. All rights reserved.

The "Two Feet of Christian Service" on handout 15 is adapted from a study sheet in *Poverty and FaithJustice*, by the Campaign for Human Development (Washington, DC: United States Conference of Catholic Bishops [USCCB], 1998), page 20 Copyright © 1998 by the USCCB, Inc. Used with permission.

The world awareness quiz and answers on handouts 16 and 17 are from *2006 Educator's Guide*, by Catholic Relief Services (CRS) (Baltimore, MD: CRS, 2005), pages 39 and 40. Copyright © 2005 by CRS. Used with permission.

The material on handout 18 is adapted from "Examination of Conscience," by Doris Donnelly, in *The Fire of Peace*, edited by Mary Lou Kownacki (Erie, PA: Pax Christi USA, 1992), pages 224–228. Copyright © 1992 by Pax Christi USA. Used with permission.

The quotations on resource 23 are from the Waging Peace Web site, *www.wagingpeace.org/menu/issues/peace-&-war/start/peace-quotes*, accessed April 5, 2006.

The song lyrics on resource 24 are adapted from "If We Are the Body," written by Mark Hall, on the Casting Crowns CD. Copyright © 2003 by Club Zoo Music/SWECS Music. All rights reserved. Used with permission of Music Services, Inc.

The prayer by Archbishop Oscar Romero on handout 19 is from the Xavierian Missionaries USA Web site, *www.xaviermissionaries.org/M_Life/NL_Archives/2003-N_Lett/Romero_Prayer.htm*, accessed April 5, 2006.

To view copyright terms and conditions for Internet materials cited here, log on to the home pages for the referenced Web sites.